A HISTORY LOVER'S GUIDE TO KANSAS CITY

PAUL KIRKMAN

Published by The History Press
Charleston, SC
www.historypress.com

First published 2020

Manufactured in the United States

ISBN 9781467144407

Library of Congress Control Number: 2020932000

CONTENTS

ACKNOWLEDGEMENTS

This book would not have been possible without the patience and restraint of my wife, Shawn Kirkman, or the knowledge and efforts of historian David W. Jackson. I admit it; I got behind schedule on this project early on. Sometimes, life just throws more at you than you expect, and you get buried. I could blame it on my other job keeping me too busy or the fact that a lot of my spare time was taken up when we moved across town—or any number of other things that everyone else has to deal with while still getting their work done. But I can't, really—not with she who knows me. I put it off and had to dig in and make up the hours late at night and in the evenings, and she had to live with a hermit for the last several weeks of the project. I put a piece of myself on the paper when I write, and it is a relief and a joy to have accomplished the task. But I didn't do it alone. So, for what it's worth, *mea culpa*, I'm sorry, and thank you, Shawn, for being there for me and taking up the slack at home when I had my face glued to a computer screen and my mind a hundred years away.

David W. Jackson, a local author and historic preservationist, started me on my path as an author fourteen years ago, when he was an archives and education director for the Jackson County (Missouri) Historical Society. As he assisted me through my college archival internship, David first tapped me to write an article for the society's journal and, then, to help with research for a history of the 1859 jail, Marshal's Home and Museum in Independence. Coauthoring with David for *LOCK DOWN: Outlaws, Lawmen and Frontier Justice in Jackson County, Missouri* inspired me to continue documenting interesting topics in local history. Since then, I've published three books; David helped edit the first two. When the deadline for this book loomed weeks away, I made a frantic call to a friend. David willingly took time out of his own projects to help provide several photographs, research and site descriptions, and he helped edit my typos, pouring out with the heightened pace. Forgive us for any errors; we did our best. Since 2000, David has added more than thirty titles to local history bookshelves, either on his own or in concert with others. He continues as a director and archivist for his consulting service, The Orderly Pack Rat, researching, writing, publishing and presenting on all facets of local history and its preservation. Thanks, David.

INTRODUCTION

So, why should a history lover care about Kansas City? After all, it's in the middle of flyover country, it's not one of the biggest cities in the United States and it's not even particularly old. But what a different country and world we would be living in without it. There would be no Mickey Mouse, Disney movies or McDonald's Happy Meals—no Pony Express, no Jesse James and no "Wild Bill" Hickok. There'd be no Teflon pans, direct dialing, Russell Stover's chocolates or Hallmark cards. Fred Astaire would have danced without Ginger Rogers, and *Gone with the Wind* would have been without Clark Gable (yes, he got his showbusiness start here). A generation wouldn't have heard Walter Cronkite report everything from the evening news to the Kennedy assassination and the moon landings. We might have never known *For Whom the Bell Tolls* or the *Old Man and the Sea* if Hemingway hadn't started his writing career at the *Kansas City Star*. There wouldn't have been a Japanese surrender on the USS *Missouri* without President Harry S. Truman, and Truman wouldn't have been a president, senator or dog catcher without the backing of Kansas City boss Tom Pendergast's political machine. Also, if Pendergast hadn't kept Kansas City wide open during Prohibition, the city's jazz scene wouldn't have spawned the Bennie Moten and Count Basie bands, and local jazz musicians, like Charlie Parker, Big Joe Turner and Pat Metheny, would not have had the chance to keep that influence moving forward for decades. Taxes would be even more taxing without Kansas City's H&R Block. Likewise, there'd be no Trans World Airlines (TWA) flying "up, up and away" or being "the most comfortable way to fly" without its headquarters in America's Heartland. Without Kansas City's Friz Freleng, we wouldn't have Bugs Bunny, Porky Pig, Tweety and Sylvester, Yosemite Sam or the Pink Panther. There would have been no *Beverly Hillbillies*, *Petticoat Junction* or *Green Acres* without Kansas City–area screenwriter Paul Henning (read *The First Hillbilly: The Untold Story of the Creator of Rural TV Comedy*, by his wife, Ruth Henning). The list goes on and on.

Kansas City is in the middle of the United States—in the middle of the nation's commerce, politics and more. The West began here, in earnest, as did the Santa Fe, Oregon and California Trails. The Lewis and Clark Trail passed by here, and the Pony Express rode from here. The first battle lines of the Civil War were formed in "Bleeding Kansas," as emigrant aid societies armed and supplied settlers (including John Brown) who were willing to do whatever they deemed necessary to stop slavery's advance. Kansas City's cowboys, outlaw gangs and larger-than-life lawmen fed into the nation's mythology, as easterners were encouraged to "go west and grow up with the country." All the while, a steady stream of immigrants was shaping the city, both literally and figuratively, as the wagons of those passing through left deep swales on the roads and those who decided to stay dug into the area's cliffs and hills. Kansas City's history, though brief when compared to other parts of the country, has been full and noteworthy, and it is an integral, inescapable part of America's story.

I feel that my biggest challenge as a history writer isn't finding a story worth telling, neither is it having to spend hours researching a topic to find something extra that makes it whole. It isn't plowing through and overcoming the inevitable case of writer's block. For me, the challenge has always been staying between the front and back covers of the book. I instinctively want to go back further, connect more dots and explore more relationships. I think if I were an artist, I would have the same sort of dilemma—needing an ever-larger canvas, because I'd want to paint what's happening just beyond the frame. Now, I find myself once again taking on a story that deserves to be told fully but in a format that requires some restraint.

A guidebook, after all, is not meant to serve as an exhaustive study but as a map and compass to help you explore an area of interest without getting lost. With this in mind, I have attempted to be efficient and sufficient in staking out a path that took hundreds of years to blaze. Kansas City grew up at the end of the river route and the head of the wagon trail to the West. The growth of the city at the river's bend is a big American story, so it naturally involves people from all over the world. To tell it right and keep it contained, I start each chapter with an introduction to an era in Kansas City's history. Next, I present the *who*, *what*, *when*, *where* and *why*, with addresses, contact information, et cetera, for the museums, locations and artifacts that are associated with that period. In this way, you can either work your way through the centuries to see Kansas City from birth to maturity or focus on only what interests you most.

To anyone who is not familiar with Kansas City history, the place can be a bit confusing. To begin with, there are two Kansas Cities: Kansas City, Kansas, and Kansas City, Missouri. Each has its own distinctive history and character, but they are only separated by an invisible line that runs down the middle of (the aptly named) State Line Road. Kansas City, Missouri, is the most-populous city in Missouri. Kansas City, Kansas, is the third-most populous city in Kansas. In addition, there is the small community of North Kansas City, on the Missouri side of the state line north of the Missouri River, with its own history. Like many large cities, Kansas City has outpaced and engulfed nearby communities, incorporating the once separate entities into a greater whole. Some of the larger communities that make up the greater Kansas City area have kept their independence (like Independence, Missouri), but many smaller towns (like Quindaro and Monticello) are just fading memories. In order to tell this city's story, even in abridged form, I am obliged to occasionally stray outside the city limits, but I will try not to wander too far into the tall grass of the prairies.

I have not attempted to include current maps of the city, as it seems somewhat superfluous in this age of technology (and continuous construction, street renaming, et cetera). However, I am a holdover from a time when asking your phone for directions was a thing of science fiction, so for the benefit of my fellow old fogeys, I would like to at least give a sense of the shape and layout of the city. I have tried to limit the area covered by this guide to an hour's drive, or sixty miles, from the city's center. The intersection of the Kansas or Kaw River and the Missouri River is where the focus of settlement began. The floodplain at the intersection came to be known as the West Bottoms, and the city's first union depot, stockyards and meatpacking industry grew up there. Early communities took hold along the south bank of the Missouri River and grew east, into the northeast neighborhood; they later spilled south, into the valley of the Blue River (a large tributary that feeds into the Missouri River from the south). The growth away from the river involved digging southward, through the cliffs and hills, toward Westport. The east–west streets were consequently numbered in ascending order to the south, which has continued into the Three Hundred Block and beyond, well past the current city limits.

People who grew up in Kansas City will talk about neighborhoods or districts like West Side, East Side, Brookside and Northeast when giving directions. Heading south from the City Market, there are so many neighborhoods and districts that even locals have a hard time keeping track of them all. From west to east, the first layer of communities south of the river include West Side, Quality Hill, the Garment District, Library District, Financial District, East Village, Paseo and Columbus Park. These are followed by West Side North, the Crossroads and the Eighteenth and Vine District. The list grows quickly from there, as the city spreads out in all directions. Old districts are revitalized, with new names like the Power and Light District, which was revitalized after the building of Sprint Center. The city's early growth and settlement followed the tributaries of the Missouri River, as farms and small communities formed along the Blue River, Brush Creek and west, along the Kansas River. The prairie extended south and west of town, and cattle and horses were rested and fed there before pushing forward on their way down or back up the western trails.

Trail towns and, later, railroad towns popped up and, sometimes, faded out as the traffic patterns changed. The older communities to the east of Kansas City pre-dated the railroads and were connected to the world by the Missouri River. Towns like Lexington, Independence and Liberty have kept their separate identities in spite of being overshadowed by their larger neighbor. Communities west of the state line include Kansas City, Kansas, Shawnee, Lenexa, Bonner Springs and Lawrence. The communities to the south include Westport (now incorporated into Kansas City), Grandview, Raytown, Belton, Mission, Prairie Village, Overland Park and Olathe. The communities to the north include North Kansas City, Riverside, Claycomo, Plattsburg, Kearney and Saint Joseph. The railroads fan out from town in all directions; the city's interstate highways include Interstate 70, running east–west; Interstate 35 and Interstate 49, running north–south; and Interstate 435, Interstate 635 and Interstate 470 that encircle large portions of the city. There are dozens of other towns and neighborhoods that could be added to the list, but the communities I have listed are all within an hour of the city's center, and many have played host to people or events that have greatly impacted the nation and the world.

The short version of all of this is that Kansas City's street numbers generally increase as you travel south. There are over one hundred little towns and several decently sized suburbs and freestanding cities that make up the Kansas City area on both sides of the state line. The highways make a skewed crosshair through the city, with Interstate 435 creating a circle and Interstates 70 and 35 crossing each other through the center. The airport is far north of downtown, and the city, which was once at the center of westward expansion, continues to be a key hub of transportation for goods and people crossing the country.

In addition to historic buildings and homes, Kansas City contains a number of museums, historic markers and parks that present and preserve the city's history. There are also a number of organizations dedicated to historic preservation that can help give depth and context to one's understanding of a particular topic or era within Kansas City's history. Kansas City also has several excellent libraries and archives that can provide resources for a further investigation of the various subjects of local history. Selected listings of these groups, locations and resources are included at the end of each chapter. They are not exhaustive, but they will get a determined visitor started. Where it was possible, I also have provided web addresses and relevant books that can supplement a reader's research.

Like I have said, it is challenging to not over-tell such a big story, but I will give you plenty of hints and resources along the way if you are like me and are moved to dig a little deeper. So, from here, you're welcome to take the full ride or jump off and ahead where you like. The trails lead in all directions, but they all connect to the city in the Heart of America: Kansas City.

1

BEND IN THE RIVER

CHEZ LES CANNES

In simple terms, it was a bend in the Missouri River that created Kansas City. Situated at the edge of an ancient inland sea, carved out by water flowing across the northern plains and shoved into place by massive glaciers, the Missouri River, the second-longest river on the North American continent, takes a sharp turn toward the east at the mouth of the Kaw along its long path toward the Mississippi River. A natural rock ledge made the juncture an easy place to land a boat or canoe, and the rich soil deposited in the surrounding floodplain ensured that abundant plant and animal life existed there. A large number of caves and springs added shelter and fresh water to the mix. The combination made the site a natural crossroads for hunters and trappers, and it eventually became the perfect place for a more permanent settlement. Stone axes that were found here date back twelve thousand years; a Native American settlement called Nebo Hill, at a site northeast of Kansas City, dates back to 3000 BCE; and as many as thirty Native American sites, including burial mounds, have been found in the area. The area's natives belong to a tribe called the Hopewell (the name came from the Hopewell farm in Ross County, Ohio, where a group of burial mounds was found), which date from around 100 BCE to 700 CE. In the following centuries, there continued to be Native American settlements in the area, but the cultures and tribes became more diverse. With the introduction of the horse and the adoption of bows and arrows, the earlier mound-building cultures were supplanted by the cultures of the plains. The Hopewell sites tended to be the homes of smaller groups, with villages rarely larger than a few dozen residents.

The first Europeans who recorded their travels to the area were Spanish, but the earliest description of the juncture of the Kansas and Missouri Rivers was written by French explorer Étienne de Veniard, Sieur de Bourgmont, in 1714. Regular trade routes and fairs had already been established among the area's Native American groups long before the arrival of European explorers, but, at opposite ends of those routes, both the French and Spanish had begun building trading posts and forts to protect their interests and develop commerce. Among these early forts were Fort Orleans (built in 1723), which was located some eighty miles east of the Kawsmouth, and Fort de Cavagnial (built in 1744), which was located near modern-day Fort Leavenworth (north of Kansas City).

Many European and American explorers passed through and noted the bend in the river where Kansas City would rise. In the late eighteenth century, Daniel Morgan Boone (son of Daniel Boone) spent time trapping and hunting in the area along the Blue River (a tributary of the Missouri). In June 1804, Captain Meriwether Lewis and Lieutenant William Clark, on their voyage of discovery, made camp in the area and explored it. Clark noted in his journal that they had reached the mouth of the Kaw on June 26, 1804, and that the area that is now known as Quality Hill in Kansas City, Missouri, was a promising location for a fort.

When Francois Chouteau (nephew of Rene Auguste Chouteau, who, along with Pierre Laclede, is credited with the founding St. Louis) chose to build a home and trading post at the river's bend and move there with his wife, Bereniece, in 1821, the foundations of Kansas City were laid. The Chouteau family had previously been in business with John Jacob Astor's American Fur Company, and, starting with Rene Auguste, had several generations of successful traders. Francois Chouteau had obtained exclusive trading rights with the tribes in the Missouri River Valley from the U.S. government. He, along with his family and employees, set up trading posts in what would become known as Bonner Springs, Turner, Argentine, Shawnee, Topeka and Lawrence on the Kansas side, and Randolph and Kansas City on the Missouri side.

Francois Chouteau brought thirty-five men to the Kawsmouth area to work in his operation, and many of them either brought families or started them with Native American women, including several members of the Blackfoot and Shawnee tribes. By the early 1830s, at least one hundred French Catholic families had settled in the area; a small catholic church was eventually built, and Father Benedict Roux came to minister to the faithful there. The Chouteau Trading Post was the center of the settlement's activity.

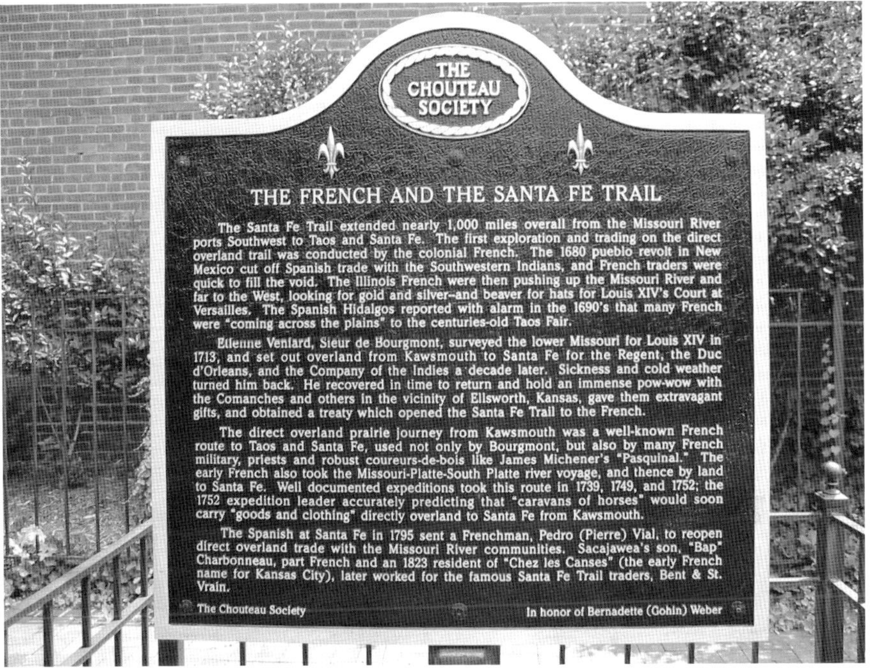

Chouteau Society marker. A tour of the original French settlement, with eleven place markers, is available through the Jackson County (Missouri) Historical Society. *Courtesy of David W. Jackson, orderlypackrat.com.*

All of the settlement's families were involved in the fur trade and most lived in the West Bottoms, near the mouth of the Kaw River. This community became known as the "French Bottoms," and the Native Americans called it "Chouteau's Town."

The community grew slowly, at first, in isolation, while the great armies and navies that served political and financial alliances competed to secure control of the center of the continent. After the War of 1812, France had little hope of competing with the British and Spanish in North America, and the other nations were forced to accept that the United States would be at least an equal partner in determining the future of the continent. But in Missouri, the French trappers, traders and missionaries were the first to establish settlements. Although the Louisiana Purchase had given the United States a legal claim to the territory, it was another thirty years before the majority of people living in the Kansas City area were actually American citizens.

The Missouri River was the lifeblood of the early settlers in Chouteau's community. Boats laden with furs gathered from around the western territories disembarked from Chouteau's landing and traveled across Missouri, to St. Louis. Trade with Mexico, along the Santa Fe Trail, built up nearby Independence, as the trade goods that had come up the Missouri River from the East were unloaded just north of the town, at Wayne's Landing. The supplies were then transferred to the hundreds of wagons that continually traversed the trail, bringing back silver, gold and incredible profits to the traders who were brave enough to make the trip. Francois Chouteau died in 1838, while he was on his way back to the Kansas City area from one such trip. Keel boats and, later, steamboats plied the river, hauling tons of cargo that had no other roads to travel on. At the time, the railroads had not made it far enough west, and the trails that had been cut through the Missouri woods had practically been grown over behind the men cutting them.

The community at the Missouri River's bend prospered, and the location was ideal—except when it wasn't, when the snowmelt from the mountains and plains hundreds of miles upstream and the summer rains would swell the river far beyond its banks. The first flood to hit the French community occurred in 1826, and it swept away the six buildings that comprised Chouteau's Trading Post on the north bank of the Missouri River. The area's next major flood occurred in 1844, and only one brick warehouse was left standing. The community never fully recovered, and the American settlers who followed struggled with the same forces of nature. The Flood of 1903 descended on a city of 160,000 people, leaving 20 dead and over 20,000 homeless. The river destroyed homes and businesses and 16 of the 17 railroad bridges in town; the stockyards and Union Depot were underwater, pulling all rail traffic to a hault. Today's Union Station was built on higher ground, at Twenty-Fifth Street and Grand Avenue, in 1914, as a response to the concern that the river would once again submerge the vital rail hub. Despite the many efforts to limit the threat that the river poses, major floods inundated the city in 1951, 1993 and 1995. The safety of the bluffs and high ground south of the river beckoned the early settlers and set the tone of growth over the ensuing years. Kansas City has always needed the river, but it cannot control it; the river reminds the city, periodically, that it is not really in charge.

There were other factors that drove the development of Kansas City. The Indian Removal Acts of the early nineteenth century had the unintended consequence of changing the economic trajectory of the small river town. In 1808, Colonel William Clark, along with a contingent of soldiers led by Nathan Boone (son of Daniel Boone), traveled overland to a spot east of the

Fort Osage National Historic Landmark, Fort Osage. *Courtesy of Wikimedia Commons.*

river's bend to build a fort overlooking the Missouri River. Fort Clark (later known as Fort Sibley and Fort Osage) was built to promote trade with the Osage, protect Americans heading west and counter the British and French influences over the area's Native American population. That same year, Pierre Chouteau negotiated a treaty with the Osage, in which they ceded seven-eighths of Missouri River and nearly half of the state of Arkansas to the United States. In the trade, the Osage were paid $1,500 and given various goods and services through Fort Clark. By 1825, the Kansa had also ceded millions of acres of territory, and by 1827, Fort Leavenworth was built to protect travelers on the Santa Fe Trail.

The combination of new lands opening up in the West and constant conflict between settlers and Native Americans in the East fueled the push for a solution to separate the two groups. In 1825, the Missouri Shawnee were the first of many tribes to be relocated to the Kansas Territory. In 1830, the Delaware were given land along the Kansas River, and in quick succession, the Ottawa, Kickapoo, Otoe, Sac and Fox tribes were moved (willingly or not) to eastern Kansas. The government's payments to the tribes were spent in the trading posts around the Kansas City area and brought wealth to the several trail towns near the river's bend. The fledgling communities' populations grew and changed rapidly in those early days.

In *The Oregon Trail*, Francis Parkman related his impressions of Independence and Westport in 1846:

> *Being at leisure one day, I rode over to Independence. The town was crowded. A multitude of shops had sprung up to furnish the emigrants and Santa Fe traders with necessaries for their journey; and there was an*

incessant hammering and banging from a dozen blacksmiths' sheds, where the heavy wagons were being repaired, and the horses and oxen shod. The streets were thronged with men, horses and mules.

Yet, a few miles closer to the Kansas Territory:

Westport was full of Indians, whose little shaggy ponies were tied by dozens along the houses and fences. Sacs and Foxes, with shaved heads and painted faces, Shawanoes and Delawares, fluttering in calico frocks, and turbans, Wyandottes dressed like white men, and a few wretched Kansas wrapped in old blankets, were strolling about the streets, or lounging in and out of the shops and houses.

These little communities continued to benefit from the abundant opportunities provided by the area; however, they were still subject to forces that they couldn't really control—from politics to the river. In spite of the challenges, they were undeterred, and homes and businesses began to take hold along the banks of the Missouri River.

RENNER-VILLAGE AT RENNER-BRENNER PARK

2901 Northwest Vivion Road
Riverside, Missouri 64150
816-741-4172
www.rennerbrennersitepark.com
www.riversidemo.com

For thousands of years, the land along Line Creek, above its juncture with the Missouri River, was inhabited by various groups of Native Americans from the Nebo Hill people and the Black Sand culture to the mound-building Hopewell and various woodland and plains tribes. Burial mounds, pottery, stone implements and thousands of other artifacts have been found in and around the site. Several monuments and informative plaques have been placed in the park, which is now in the National Register of Historic Places. The park is maintained by the City of Riverside, Missouri, and is ADA approved, with parking available. The park also has a walking trail, restrooms, drinking fountains, a skating park and a shelter house.

KAW POINT PARK

1403 Fairfax Trafficway
Kansas City, Kansas 66115
www.lewisandclarkwyco.org
www.lewisandclarkkc.org

In June 1804, Lewis and Clark's voyage of discovery made camp at the confluence of the Kaw and Missouri Rivers; they stayed in the area for three days to explore, make repairs and hunt. The park is now in the heart of Kansas City, and the campground's location has a good view of downtown. An open-air education pavilion flies the flags of nineteen regional tribes and has interpretive signs and a plaque commemorating the events of the Lewis and Clark expedition's visit. The site's natural rock encampment theater is made of limestone benches engraved with the names of the expedition's crew (including Lewis' Newfoundland dog, Seaman). The park has paved hiking and biking trails; statues of Lewis and Clark, Sacagawea and her child, Clark's slave named York and Seaman; and a nice view of the rivers.

FORT OSAGE NATIONAL HISTORIC LANDMARK

107 Osage Street
Sibley, Missouri 64088
816-650-3278
www.fortosagenhs.com
www.makeyourdayhere.com/205/Fort-Osage

This National Historic Landmark was reconstructed in the 1940s; it was built from the original plans and on the original fort's foundations. Work on Fort Clark (sometimes Fort Sibley and, later, Fort Osage) started on September 5, 1808, under the direction of William Clark, who had noted the location four years earlier on his voyage of discovery. Clark and a detachment of soldiers returned to the location, guided by Nathan Boone, as part of an effort by the U.S. government to expand trade and increase its military presence in the newly acquired western territory. The site consists of several log buildings, including blockhouses, officer and enlisted quarters, a trading post or factory and as a modern education center. The education center includes a gift shop, museum, exhibit space and an auditorium; the building also has a good view of the fort and the Missouri River.

DANIEL MORGAN BOONE PARK AND BOONE-HAYES CEMETERY

2100 East Sixty-Third Street
(Corner of Sixty-Third and Euclid Streets)
Kansas City, Missouri 64130
www.kcparks.org
www.nsdkc.org

Daniel Morgan Boone was the first of many descendants of Daniel Boone to visit the Kansas City area. Morgan Boone spent time trapping along the Big Blue River in the late eighteenth century, and, then, settled near St. Charles, where his famous father and brothers followed. He served as a captain in the Missouri Mounted Militia in the War of 1812 and was involved in a number of businesses in the territory's early years. Boone moved near what became Lawrence, Kansas, in 1825. He also bought a large tract of land at Sixty-Third Street and Holmes Road in 1831, where he and his family lived. In 1836, Boone sold part of the land to his nephew Boone Hayes. Daniel Morgan Boone died of cholera in 1839 and was buried alongside his wife, Sarah Lewis Boone, and other Boone descendants in the family's cemetery (today, a fourteen-acre park). Hundreds of other family burial grounds and larger municipal cemeteries dot the metro, where Kansas City's pioneers rest in peace.

NELSON-ATKINS MUSEUM OF ART

4525 Oak Street
Kansas City, Missouri 64111
www.nelson-atkins.org

It took a few years, but the mega estates of William Rockhill Nelson, the founder of the *Kansas City Star*, and Mary McAfee Atkins, a schoolteacher-turned-philanthropist, followed through with their benefactors wishes to create a supreme pubic art museum. The 1933 monolith of the Nelson-Atkins Museum of Art was constructed on the site of Nelson's former home, and they had plenty of money to build the nucleus of their collections through the Great Depression.

Nelson-Atkins Museum of Art. Native American beadwork, pottery and other crafts are among the exhibits at this popular Kansas City museum. *Courtesy of Carol M. Highsmith's America, Library of Congress, Prints and Photographs Division (LC-DIG-highsm-04151).*

The Native American collection of art at the Nelson-Atkins Museum of Art is displayed in a suite of three galleries, with over two hundred objects in a variety of mediums (pottery, textiles, sculpture, et cetera). In addition to the outstanding permanent displays, the museum has a variety of special exhibitions periodically brought in, including many that help connect art to history (for example, "Golden Prospects," a winter 2019 exhibition of daguerreotypes from the California gold rush era). Nelson-Atkins's collections connect to every era of the region's history. The museum should make any history lover's short list for a visit to Kansas City.

NATIONAL ARCHIVES AT KANSAS CITY

400 West Pershing RoadKansas City, Missouri 64108
816-268-8072
www.archives.gov/kansas-city

One of a handful of regional branches of the nation's federal archival repositories, the National Archives at Kansas City offers researchers a boon of resources from agencies across seven Midwestern states. The archives also have a variety of resources for genealogical and historical studies focused on specific populations, including African Americans, aliens (foreigners, not the outer-space kind) and Chinese immigrants. The archives also have resources for historical studies of labor and employment, the land and environment, national parks, Native Americans, naturalizations, the New Deal and Great Depression and Veteran-related records—just to name a few.

JACKSON COUNTY (MISSOURI) HISTORICAL SOCIETY AND THE CHOUTEAU SOCIETY

112 West Lexington Avenue
Independence, Missouri 64050
816-252-7454
jchs.org

The offices, archives, research library and bookstore of this excellent organization and research resource are located in the historic Truman Jackson County Courthouse on Independence Square. The Jackson County Historical Society (JCHS) also owns and operates the 1859 Jail, Marshal's Home and Museum (217 North Main Street), where Jesse James's gang members and the guerrilla soldier William Clarke Quantrill were incarcerated. The Chouteau Society, administered by JCHS, was formed here in 1984, with the purpose of "collecting, preserving and disseminating information relating to the French heritage of the New World, the Midwest and, with particular and special emphasis upon, metropolitan Kansas City, Missouri and Kansas for the period extending from and after the year 1599 Anno Domini." A series of eleven markers have been placed by the group, and a tour of the historic locations can be found on the society's website.

THE NATIVE SONS AND DAUGHTERS OF GREATER KANSAS CITY

PO Box 26071
Overland Park, Kansas 66225
913-207-3310
www.nsdkc.org

This local, member-driven organization is dedicated to preserving the heritage of the Kansas City, Missouri community. Leading through advocacy, education and restoration activities, maintaining and preserving archives, placing historic markers and presenting programs through its speaker's bureau, the group has been active since the 1930s. The Native Sons and Daughters of Kansas City is another great resource for information on your personal voyage to discover Kansas City. Their extensive archives are available through the State Historical Society of Missouri, Kansas City Research Center on the campus of the University of Missouri, Kansas City. They can be found online at www.shs.umsystem.edu/kansascity/manuscripts/k0279.pdf.

Read More

Across the Wide Missouri, by Bernard DeVoto
American Paintings: The Collections of the Nelson-Atkins Museum of Art, by Margaret C. Conrads
At the River's Bend: An Illustrated History of Kansas City, Independence and Jackson County, by Sherry Schirmer
Before Lewis and Clark: The Story of the Chouteaus, the French Dynasty That Ruled America's Frontier, by Shirley Christian
Boss Busters and Sin Hounds: Kansas City and Its Star, by Harry Haskell
Cher Oncle, Cher Papa: The Letters of Francois and Berenice Chouteau, by Dorothy Brandt Marra and David Boutros
The Chouteaus: First Family of the Fur Trade, by Stan Hoig
Elmwood Cemetery: Stories of Kanas City, by Bruce Mathews and Anne Sutton Canfield

Fort Osage: A History of Its First Occupation, 1808–1813, by Michael L. Gillespie

Frontiersman: Daniel Boone and the Making of America, by Meredith Mason Brown

Great Plains Originals: Documents from America's Heartland, by Brian Burnes

Images of America: Early Kansas City, Missouri, by Leigh Ann Little and John M. Olinskey

Jackson County Pioneers, by Pearl Wilcox

The Journals of Lewis and Clark, by Meriwether Lewis and William Clark

Kansas City Chronicles: An Up-to-Date History, by David W. Jackson

Kansas City: An American Story, by Rick Montgomery, Shirl Kasper, Jean Dodd, Monroe Dodd, David Eams and Arthur S. Brisbane

Kansas City's Historic Union Cemetery, by Bruce Matthews and Judity King

Lost Souls of the Lost Township, by Paul R. Petersen and David W. Jackson

Missouri: Crossroads of the Nation by Charles Phillips and Betty Burnett

My Father, Daniel Boone, by Neal O. Hammon

The Nelson-Atkins Museum of Art: A Handbook of the Collection, by Marc F. Wilson et al.

Nelson-Atkins Museum of Art: A History, by Kristie C. Wolferman

Seeking a Newer World: The Fort Osage Journals and Letters of George Sibley, 1808–1811, by Jeffrey E. Smith

Winding the Clock on the Independence Square: Jackson County's Historic Truman Courthouse, by David W. Jackson

Your Land, Our Land: Two Centuries of American Words and Images from the Regions of the National Archives, by Monroe Dodd and Brian Burnes

2

TRAPPERS, TRADERS AND OUTFITTERS

At the dawn of the nineteenth century, the vast majority of the Missouri Territory's residents were Native Americans. In the late eighteenth century, Spanish authorities offered land to Americans, like Daniel Boone and his family, if they moved into the eastern portions of the territory (where Boone spent the last twenty years of his life). When the territory changed hands and Napoleon Bonaparte decided to sell it all to the United States, the trickle of American settlers rapidly increased to a flood.

Within two decades, large numbers of trappers, miners and farmers settled the eastern portion of the state, up and down the Mississippi River and west along the Missouri River. Many of the Missouri Territory's American settlers, like the Boones, came from the South and brought slaves with them. Tobacco and hemp farms along the Missouri River extended slavery north of its traditional boundaries. A bitter fight to contain the practice was halted by the 1820 Missouri Compromise, which led to Missouri's recognition as a state. The War of 1812 split alliances among the state's Native Americans, and the treaties that followed generally were lopsided affairs that involved large parcels of land being exchanged for minimal payments and worse land to the west (often at gunpoint or, at least, under threat).

In 1830, the Indian Removal Act gave President Andrew Jackson the authority to negotiate treaties with Native American tribes living in the South; in his negotiations, Jackson offered them land in the West in exchange for the lands they were living on at the time. The tribes that refused to move were forcibly removed by the army, and horrific hardships and loss of life resulted from the policy. Tribes that had previously thrived in the eastern forests, where game and water were plentiful, were pushed into what was described as the Great American Desert.

Both the expansion of slavery and the forced migration of Native American tribes contributed to the growth and development of the Kansas City area. Nearby towns, like Lexington, Liberty, and Independence, formed in the 1820s and had large populations of slave owners and slaves. Jackson County, Missouri, was named after Tennessee's Andrew Jackson, who was popular with the many southern transplants in the area well before he was elected president. Independence was designated as the county seat in 1827, and in the same year, a log courthouse was built in the town using slave labor. The 1827 Log Courthouse still stands at 107 West Kansas Street in Independence and is a museum maintained by the city.

The trading posts near the territories where tribes of Native Americans had been moved grew into towns like Westport, Wyandotte, Shawnee and Bonner Springs. Military posts and connecting trails and roads were built ostensibly to keep settlers and the Native Americans protected from one another. Fort Leavenworth was built in 1827, and Fort Scott was built in 1842.

Log Jackson County Courthouse, circa 1827, Independence, Missouri. *Courtesy of Paul Kirkman.*

Fort Leavenworth (about thirty-five miles north of downtown Kansas City) in Leavenworth, Kansas, is the oldest active army post west of the Mississippi. Colonel Henry Leavenworth, along with the officers and men of the Third Infantry Regiment from Jefferson Barracks at St. Louis, Missouri, established Fort Leavenworth in 1827. It was built as a forward base to protect the Santa Fe Trail. The first army installation in Cantonment Leavenworth (its original name) comprised 14 officers and 174 enlisted men. The cantonment grew in importance after the Indian Removal Act of 1830 and as traffic on the Santa Fe and Oregon Trails increased. In 1832, Cantonment Leavenworth was renamed Fort Leavenworth, and between 1832 and 1834, the rookery was built as living quarters for the fort's unmarried officers. The rookery is the oldest building in Kansas and served as the office of the first territorial governor from 1854 to 1855. With Leavenworth men serving in the Indian wars, the Mexican-American War, the Mormon War, Bleeding Kansas, the Civil War and beyond, the fort has a long and storied history, and there are monuments and a museum on the base to help tell it.

Before the arrival of the army, the tradesmen and settlers of the Kansas City area had been trappers and mountain men. One name in particular looms large in both Kansas City history and the history of the development of the West: Jim Bridger. Born James Felix Bridger in 1804, Jim was a mountain man, trapper, army scout and guide who explored and trapped all over the western territories in the first half of the nineteenth century. In 1822, at the age of eighteen, Bridger joined General William Henry Ashley's fur-trapping expedition to the upper part of the Missouri River. The party, later called Ashley's Hundred, included Jedediah Smith and many others who later became famous mountain men and formed the Rocky Mountain Fur Company. Bridger was a contemporary of many early famous explorers of the West, and he knew many of them, including Jedediah Smith, Kit Carson, John Frémont, Robert Campbell and William Sublette (the latter two also lived in the Kansas City area). Over the course of twenty years, Bridger joined and led numerous expeditions to explore and map the West for commercial, government and military purposes. Although Bridger was illiterate, he could converse in French, Spanish and several native languages well enough to mediate disputes between Native American tribes and settlers. In 1843, Bridger established Fort Bridger in Wyoming to serve as a supply point for the Oregon Trail, but after the Mormon War in Utah, he sold out and moved back to Westport.

In 1853, Bridger purchased land south of Kansas City. Bridger's farm stretched as far north as Watts Mill and as far south as Red Bridge. In New

Santa Fe, he became a partner in the trading post of Vasquez, Bridger and Watts. The Watts in the partnership was Josiah, one of the sons of Anthony Watts, who owned Watts Mill. The post was successful in selling supplies and making small loans to settlers and travelers. Bridger continued to work occasionally as a scout, but he made the Kansas City area his home base. Bridger was known for his storytelling, and although he was one of the first Americans to see many of the wonders of the West (like the geysers at Yellowstone and the Great Salt Lake), he enjoyed telling tall tales. Bridger claimed to have seen a petrified forest and then added petrified birds to his story. Another of his tales involved him being trapped and surrounded by Cheyenne warriors. When telling the story, he would pause and wait for the listener to ask what happened and would then gravely tell them, "I got killed, of course."

In 1866, Bridger bought a tavern in Westport, at 504 Westport Road; in 2019, it was still a tavern and club that had aptly been named Bridger's. In 1881, Jim Bridger died and was buried on a hill in the Watts Burial Ground that is a half mile north of Watts Mill (101st and Jefferson Streets). He was later removed and reinterred at Mount Washington Cemetery, where his granite headstone, purportedly sourced from the Rocky Mountains, marks his final resting place. Jim Bridger is honored, along with Pony Express founder Alexander Majors and Kansas City founder John Calvin McCoy, in a sculpture at Pioneer Square in Westport. The Independence School District named a middle school after Bridger, and its faculty members and students raised the funds to place a second Bridger statue at the National Frontier Trails Museum in Independence. Bridger's likeness is also on one of the ten memorial column panels that were placed on the new (2011) Red Bridge, marking the area where all of the three westward trails (Santa Fe, California and Oregon) intersected and crossed the Big Blue River (North of Minor Park, where you can see wagon swales and the Old Red Bridge).

The Shawnee name is ubiquitous in the Kansas City area; there are several Shawnee Mission High Schools, the town of Shawnee, Shawnee Mission Parkway, et cetera. The Shawnee were among the first tribes to be removed to the Kansas Territory, and many of the descendants of those early survivors still live in the area. One of the many Shawnee who moved to Kansas City was Tenskwatawa, a Shawnee religious and political leader known as the "Prophet," who was the younger brother of the Shawnee warrior chief Tecumseh. The two organized a Native American federation that was led by Tecumseh against the United States in 1811. Tecumseh later allied with the British in the War of 1812, but he was killed during battle. Tenskwatawa went into exile in Canada for many years. In 1826, Tenskwatawa helped establish a village in Kansas City, Kansas. By 1833, only the Black Bob band of the Shawnee still resisted the United States' relocation efforts. The Shawnee finally settled in northeastern Kansas, near Olathe and Gum Springs, along the Kansas River in Monticello. Tenskwatawa died in 1836, on Shawnee land, within the Argentine community of Kansas City, Kansas. Some of the Shawnee later intermarried with the nonnative settlers of Kansas City and were able to keep some of the land they had received when they were first moved to the area. Some groups (like the Black Bob tribe) fought lengthy court battles over the land that was taken from them (especially during the Civil War). Other groups moved on to the Oklahoma Territory.

Local merchants competed for army contracts as well as the annual payments that were received by uprooted tribes, who had few choices as to where to spend the money that was given to them. Missionaries came to the area along with, if not ahead of, other settlers. Reverend Isaac McCoy was a Baptist missionary and leader of the Indian Removal movement. He argued that moving the eastern tribes far from white settlements, whiskey traders and other unscrupulous businessmen was the only way to keep them safe. He lobbied for the government to provide reservation lands in the West, and he led survey teams that laid out reservations in Kansas and Oklahoma. On these surveys, he brought out representatives from several tribes in the hope of creating a separate territory just for Native Americans. When the Shawnee and Delaware tribes moved to the Kansas City area, Isaac McCoy and his wife, Christiana (Polke) McCoy, followed, bringing their son, John Calvin McCoy; daughter, Delilah; and her husband, Johnston Lykins. In 1833, John Calvin McCoy built a cabin and trading post at what is now 444 Westport Road (at the northeast corner of the intersection of Westport Road and Pennsylvania Avenue) near the state line, and built a town around, which he dubbed West Port.

Johnston Lykins purchased land in Kansas City and worked in various positions as a missionary, self-taught doctor, translator and political figure. He was the first president of Kansas City's city council and the town's second mayor. Daniel Yocum later moved to the area from Tennessee and built a log house at the northwest corner of Westport Road and Mill Street, which he opened as the first tavern in Westport. In the town's early days, John Calvin McCoy had trouble selling lots in his little community. But a saddler set up shop there, and a few others, hoping to capitalize on the trail traffic, eventually moved in. As Westport slowly grew, McCoy made the astute decision to widen the river road and connect his little town to the landing. He even convinced steamboat captains to bypass Independence and drop off supplies for his store at his warehouse near the river. Once the steamboats started making the trip to haul freight to the area, it didn't take long for them to start bringing passengers, who came to start out on the trails that were a little farther west.

Moses Grinter was another early transplant to the Kansas Territory. In 1828, he was stationed as a soldier at Fort Leavenworth, and in 1831, he was appointed by the government to operate a ferry on the north bank of the Kaw River in the Delaware Reservation. While he was stationed there, Grinter met his future wife, Windagamen "Annie" Marshall, who was half-Delaware. They were married in 1838. The Grinters operated the ferry and a trading post near the military road that linked Forts Scott and Leavenworth. Their home, which was built in 1857, is now a museum run by the Kansas State Historical Society.

The Shawnee Methodist Indian Mission was established in 1830 at the request of the "Fish" tribe of the Shawnee, which had been removed from Ohio and initially set up in Turner, Kansas. Reverend Thomas Johnson (the namesake of Johnson County) eventually moved the mission to Fairway, Kansas, in 1839, and established a manual training school there. The majority of students who attended the school during its years of operation (1839–1862) were members of the Shawnee and Delaware tribes. Three of the oldest buildings in the state of Kansas remain on the site of the Shawnee Indian Mission, which is now a Kansas State Historic Site that is operated by the Kansas Historical Society in cooperation with the City of Fairway, Kansas.

The seemingly boundless opportunities that the West presented to American settlers were constant draws to the desperate and the bold. Trappers and pioneers began moving their families into the farthest reaches of the continent and often served as guides and hosts to new arrivals coming up the trails. Groups of pioneers heading for the Oregon Territory started following the trappers routes from Independence as early as 1836; the Bartleson-Bidwell Party left Westport for California in 1841.

Thousands followed in their footsteps, which led up from the river, into Independence and Westport and out onto the plains. Andrew Drips worked for the American Fur Company before he was appointed as an Indian agent in Northern Missouri. His wife, Mary, was a member of the Oto tribe, and they built a home on the high ground south of Quality Hill (near today's Thirteenth Street). Parts of their land was later sold in lots, and the area became known as Mulkey Square. Today, it is part of the resurgent west

Town of Kansas painting, circa 1935. *Courtesy of Frederick Emanuel Shane, Library of Congress, Prints and Photographs Division (LC-DIG-highsm-11046).*

Home of Moses and Annie Grinter, Grinter Place State Historic Site. *Courtesy of Wikimedia Commons.*

Shawnee Methodist Mission, east building, Kansas City, Wyandotte County, Kansas. *Courtesy of the Library of Congress Prints and Photographs Division (HABS KANS,46-_1B-).*

side of town that includes the Kauffman Center for the Performing Arts. The Dripses' daughter, Catherine (Drips) Mulkey, gave some of their land to Kansas City in 1882, to be used as the city's first public park.

In 1833, John Bartleston erected a cabin in the woods, a good day's travel down the Santa Fe Trail from Westport Landing. Settlers soon began stopping at the cabin, and the community of New Santa Fe grew up around his farm. The town was incorporated in the 1850s, but it declined steadily as the Border War, Civil War and, finally, the railroads drove people and trade away. Today, a cemetery and the Trailside Center, managed by the New Santa Fe Historical Society and Kansas City's Parks Department, remain to mark the town's former location.

In 1836, Archibald Rice moved eight miles down the Santa Fe Trail, to an area south of Independence and Westport. There, he built a home and three slave cabins. He also built a campsite and sold supplies and produce from his farm to the many groups that were starting their westward treks. Many kind words were written in pioneer diaries of the Rice family's hospitality. The farm home, completed in 1844, still stands and represents one of the quandaries of historic preservation: whether we should preserve and how to preserve and present sites with a morally mixed history. Rice was a slave owner and built his home on land that, one could argue, was unfairly obtained by the U.S. government from Native Americans. The home survived the Border War and the Civil War and has architectural and historical significance. One of the Rice family's slaves was Sophie White; a replica of the cabin she lived in, both as a slave and as an emancipated person, sits on the property. The City of Raytown and the Friends of the Rice-Tremonti Home are tasked with preserving a home tied to events and people that have both positive and negative connotations; it is worth noting that they have worked to keep the memories of both alive.

Seth Edmund Ward was a trader on the California, Oregon and Santa Fe Trails; he parlayed his success into a real estate empire, some of which is a part of today's Country Club District in Kansas City, Missouri. As a young man, Ward moved to Independence, Missouri, where he was hired by Lancaster P. Lupton as a trapper for his company in Colorado; from there, Ward traveled to Fort Lupton, Colorado. In 1848, with the collapse of the fur trade business, Ward went into business with William Guerrier; the firm of Ward and Guerrier provided supplies for settlers in Colorado and Wyoming. Ward and Guerrier were commissioned to be the official sutlers (sanctioned civilian merchants to military posts) of Fort Laramie, giving them a monopoly on the frontier. In 1860, Ward married Mary Frances McCarty,

Rice-Tremonti Home and Aunt Sophie's slave cabin, Raytown, Missouri. *Courtesy of Wikimedia Commons.*

the daughter of Colonel John Harris of Westport, and they eventually moved to Nebraska City, Nebraska, in 1863. In 1871, Ward moved to Kansas City, where he bought the 450-acre farm of his friend and fellow trader William Bent. The farm ran from State Line to Wornall Roads, and from Fifty-First to Fifty-Fifth Streets. In 1897, Ward leased the east pasture to the Kansas City Country Club to be used as the town's first golf course; his son, Hugh, was a founding member of the country club. Seth Ward passed away in 1904, and his son, Hugh, followed in 1908. In 1925, Hugh Ward's widow sold the land to the widow of Jacob Loose, who used it to create a park. The original farm, where part of the Battle of Westport was fought, is now known as Loose Park.

The Missouri River's bend put Kansas City on the map, as did the trails that connected it to the West. But the steamboat connected the city to the rest of the country and the world. In 1832, the steamboat *John Hancock* dropped the first load destined for John McCoy's store off at the landing on the end of Grand Avenue in Kansas City. Within a few years, the landing saw steamboats by the dozens, dropping people off, heading west, picking

Display of recovered artifacts at the Steamboat Arabia Museum. *Courtesy of David W. Jackson, coauthor of* Fueling Change: The Once and Future Kanas City, *orderlypackrat.com.*

up produce and heading east. In the 1840s, warehouses and homes sprang up both in Westport and along the riverfront. By the end of the decade, nearly twenty boats docked at the levee every week, each navigating the unpredictable and dangerous waters between St. Louis and Kansas City.

In 1856, the steamboat *Arabia* was lost in those waters, along with the two hundred tons of cargo that it was carrying onboard. After 132 years, the *Arabia* was found with much of its cargo intact, buried beneath a cornfield, where the river once ran deep. The *Arabia* Steamboat Museum, located in the historic City Market, presents the ship's bounty of goods and reminds visitors of the dangers that were faced by those who served onboard. However, the twists, turns, snags and sawyers of the river were not enough to discourage the pioneers or to stop the flow of people and goods traveling down the river. Boats plied their way to St. Joseph, Missouri, and hauled cargo up the Missouri River—as far as Montana—in the 1860s. The towns that had access to the river prospered and grew, and the trails beyond the river depended on the steamboats to maintain their flows of cash, settlers and produce. Towns like Weston and Lexington shipped tobacco and hemp back down the river, and the goods that came back up the trails from the forests and mines of the West made their way to the East Coast and beyond.

JIM BRIDGER'S GRAVE

Mount Washington Cemetery
614 South Brookside Avenue
Independence, Missouri
www.findagrave.com/memorial/134/jim-bridger

ISAAC MCCOY MARKER

4401 Wornall Road
Kansas City, Missouri 64111

In the courtyard near the chapel at St. Luke's Hospital, this marker honors Baptist missionary Isaac McCoy as one of the earliest settlers in the territory. Two of Isaac's children were John Calvin McCoy and Delilah McCoy; she later married Dr. Johnston Lykins. All of the McCoys were key figures in the early days of Kansas City. Isaac McCoy was a controversial figure who strongly advocated for a separate territory for Native American tribes, where they could be safe from white encroachment and live in peace. After the Indian Removal Acts, he made surveys of the Kansas Territory and tried to help with resettlement. The Isaac McCoy family lived around Forty-Third Street and Wornall Road, on a homestead called Locust Hill (named after an ancient grove of locust trees), which overlooked Mill Creek Valley, south of Westport, where the Kansas City Country Club Plaza was later built.

SHAWNEE INDIAN MISSION STATE HISTORIC SITE

3403 West Fifty-Third Street
Fairway, Kansas 6620
913-262-0867
www.kshs.orgfairwaykansas.org

The Shawnee Methodist Mission was established by the Reverend Thomas Johnson in Turner, Kansas, in 1830, after the Shawnee tribe had been forcibly moved to the area. In 1839, the mission was moved to its current location in Fairway, Kansas, where the first brick building and manual labor training school was built. The mission continued to serve as a boarding school for the members of several Native American tribes, but the students were primarily members of the Shawnee and Delaware tribes. Travelers on the Santa Fe and Oregon Trails would stop and get supplies at the school. The Kansas Territorial Legislature temporarily relocated to the site in 1855, and Union soldiers camped there during the Civil War. The site includes three buildings, with period-decorated rooms, displays, guided tours and a video.

GRINTER PLACE STATE HISTORIC SITE

1420 South Seventy-Eighth Street
Muncie, Kansas 66111
913-299-0373
kshs.grinter@ks.gov

One of the Kansas Territory's earliest arrivals, Moses Grinter, and his wife, Annie, a Lenape-Delaware Native American, operated a ferry and a trading post that served the new reservations and military traffic from Fort Leavenworth (where Grinter had served as a soldier). Overlooking the historic Delaware Crossing on the Kansas River, the Grinters' two-story redbrick house was built in 1857, and it is the oldest home in Wyandotte County. The Kansas State Historical Society administers the historic home, museum and gift shop. The rooms have period furnishings and some of the Grinters' personal belongings on display.

1827 LOG COURTHOUSE

107 West Kansas Avenue
Independence, Missouri 64050
816-325-7111
www.visitindependence.com/listings/1827-log-courthouse

Built by slaves in 1827, the Log Courthouse was Jackson County's first, temporary courthouse. In 1836, it was decommissioned, and the county relocated to its court operations to a permanent brick courthouse on Independence Square. The log structure was then used as a mercantile store by Mormons. After being occupied by the county again in 1932, county executive Harry S. Truman used the building while the Jackson County Courthouse on the Square was being remodeled. It is rumored that a slave auction block was buried in the Log Courthouse's front yard, perhaps to mark the passing of the building's connection to the pre-emancipation period. The old cabin stood while thousands of emigrants passed through the town square and battles and raids raged during the Civil War, and it even survived after it was taken off its original foundation and moved to its current location. Now, the almost-two-hundred-year-old structure continues to serve the community as a museum that is administered by the City of Independence. Jackson County's other nineteenth-century courthouse, the Truman Courthouse, is located just one block north.

SHOAL CREEK LIVING HISTORY MUSEUM

7000 Northeast Barry Road
Kansas City, Missouri 64156
816-792-2655
www.shoalcreeklivinghistorymuseum.com

Owned by Kansas City Parks, Recreation and Boulevards and operated by the Shoal Creek Association, the Shoal Creek Living History Museum contains seventeen authentic nineteenth-century buildings dating from 1807 to 1885. Its historic log cabins and homes were relocated from surrounding counties and, along with reenactors, re-creates life in a nineteenth-century village. School tours, weddings and Victorian teas at the Thornton Mansion are among the services available through the museum. Be sure to check its website for its special event schedule before planning a visit.

PIONEER TRAILS ADVENTURES

217 North Main Street
Independence, Missouri 64050
816-254-2466
pta.mules@yahoo.com

Over the past twenty years, this service has become a mainstay around the historic Independence Square. Cowboy hat–wearing guides give wagon rides, pulled by Missouri mules, through history. There are more historic sites within a short trot's distance of Independence Square than even proprietor Ralph Goldsmith could have imagined when he first hitched up his team here. In addition to his regular route, special historic tours and multi-wagon tours are also available. The tour adjusts with the weather and holidays, so don't be surprised if you notice the mules have sprouted reindeer horns in December.

CAVE SPRING NATIONAL HISTORIC SITE

8701 East Gregory Boulevard
Kansas City, Missouri 64133
816-659-1945
www.kshs.org

At one time, the area around Cave Spring Park was a heavily traveled junction on the Santa Fe Trail known as the Barnes Enclosure. Later, the Oregon and California Trails also passed by this location. Harry Truman's maternal grandfather, Solomon Young, owned Cave Spring in the 1870s, and it was a popular stop for local youth and travelers during the late nineteenth century. In the 1920s, part of the land was used as an Army Air Corps reserve airport that was dubbed Richards Flying Field after local World War I pilot John Francisco Richards II who was killed in action. This was Kansas City's first air terminal; a golf course and cabins on the property drew visitors to the area between 1926 and the 1940s. Formally known as William M. Klein Park, Cave Spring is now a thirty-nine-acre site with a small museum and exhibit hall. The site has five miles of hiking trails and, yes, a cave with a spring.

RAYTOWN HISTORICAL SOCIETY MUSEUM

9705 East Sixty-Third Street
Raytown, Missouri 64133
816-353-5033
www.raytownhistoricalsociety.org

Among the permanent exhibits at the Raytown Historical Society Museum is a display of a blacksmith shop. This display is appropriate since the town was named after blacksmith William Ray, who built his shop on the Santa Fe Trail to attract business from the many travelers heading west on the first legs of their cross-country trips. The community that grew up around the shop adopted his name. Raytown is now a large and busy suburb of Kansas City; it is located south of Independence, near the Truman Sports Complex.

TRAILSIDE CENTER

9901 Holmes Street
Kansas City, Missouri 64131
816-942-3581
www.trailsidecenter.org

HISTORICAL SOCIETY OF NEW SANTA FE

122nd Street and State Line Road
Kansas City, Missouri 64145
www.newsantafe.org

The town of New Santa Fe stood at the intersection of State Line Road and the Santa Fe Trail. The community developed around the farm of John Bartleston, who built a cabin in the woods alongside the Santa Fe Trail in 1833. The town started off with high hopes, relying on the busy trail traffic that left the wagon swales still exist today. In 1851, the Lipscomb family laid out the town, but the Border War and Civil War devastated the area, and the railroad bypassed the community, leaving a cemetery without a real town. The Historical Society of New Santa Fe assists the staff of the Trailside Center in maintaining the cemetery, and it provides information for those interested in the era of Westward Expansion.

THE *ARABIA* STEAMBOAT MUSEUM

400 Grand Avenue
Kansas City, Missouri 64106
816-471-1856
www.1856.com

Before the rise of the railroad, rivers were the only way to move large amounts of cargo through the wilderness. In the early nineteenth century, every year, hundreds of steamboats would make the treacherous ascent up the muddy Missouri River to the landing in Kansas City and beyond. After carrying thousands of passengers, loads of livestock and manufactured goods to the river's busy markets, over four hundred steamboats met their ends in the river's depths. In September 1856, the Steamboat *Arabia* set out on a routine mission but was soon torn open by a snag just six miles past Kansas City. There were no casualties, save one mule. The boat was pushed too far into the mud to save, and as the hours passed, the river buried it deeper. Over time, the river changed course, but the *Arabia* remained, buried forty-five feet underground, with its two hundred tons of cargo remarkably intact. After 132 years, the *Arabia* was found and unearthed; its contents were put on display at the *Arabia* Steamboat Museum in the popular River Market. The items found onboard, which ranged from fine china to the world's oldest pickles, make the museum a fun and fascinating stop.

WESTON HISTORICAL MUSEUM

601 Main Street
Weston, Missouri 64098
816-386-2977
www.westonhistoricalmuseum.org

Whole towns are not normally on lists of historic sites, but it would be remiss to leave the little town of Weston out of this section. As early as 1836, Weston was already an established river port and jumping off point for the Santa Fe Trail. At one time, it had the largest population in the state and could claim Buffalo Bill Cody as a resident. In 1850, over two hundred steamboats docked at the port of Weston, and the city rivaled Kansas City and St. Joseph for river traffic. By the 1880s, the river channel had shifted away from the town, and its neighbors dwarfed it in size, but Weston has continued to thrive and has even become a tourist destination. This may be due, in part, to the 160-year-old McCormick Distillery, the Weston Brewery and a collection of antique shops in the historic downtown area (where there are also several buildings that are over 140 years old in the sixteen-block national historic district). The Weston Historical Museum also serves to introduce visitors to the community. While the author of this book has tried to limit the guide's scope to a fifty-mile radius of downtown Kansas City, Weston, like many of the communities that make up the greater Kansas City area, fortunately falls well within that limitation and could serve as a daytrip destination for readers who want to explore Kansas City's outer limits.

RICE-TREMONTI HOME

8801 East Sixty-Sixth Street
Raytown, Missouri 64133
816-358-7423 • 816-510-8179
www.rice-tremonti.org

Though this historic home does not have a regular tour, the Friends of the Rice-Tremonti Home Association holds a variety of events that open the house to the public every year. Just a glimpse of the surviving 1840s plantation home is worth the drive. Homes like this are rare in these parts, because most antebellum homes in Jackson County were burned to the ground in 1863, after the issue of Order No. 11 during the Civil War.

FORT LEAVENWORTH AND THE FRONTIER ARMY MUSEUM

100 Reynolds Avenue
Fort Leavenworth, Kansas 66027
913-684-3186
www.armyupress.army.mil/Educational-Services/Frontier-Army-Museum

Established in 1827, Fort Leavenworth in Leavenworth, Kansas, is the oldest active army post west of the Mississippi. The Frontier Army Museum's main gallery depicts the important role the army had in the protection, expansion and development of the West. The museum's displays show some of the tools of the trade and follow the history of the post through the modern era. The fort is the home of the only U.S. military maximum-security prisons, the U.S. Army Command and General Staff College (graduates include George S. Patton, Omar N. Bradley and Dwight D. Eisenhower) and the Fort Leavenworth National Cemetery, which contains over thirty thousand graves of veterans and dependents going back to the 1840s, including two-time Medal of Honor recipient Thomas Ward Custer, who died with his brother, George Armstrong Custer, at the Battle of Little Big Horn.

SETH EAST WARD HOME (PRIVATE RESIDENCE)

1032 West Fifty-Fifth Street
Kansas City, Missouri

The land of the Seth E. Ward Home has passed through many hands, including early Mormon settlers, until William W. Bent bought the property in 1858. He built a two-story brick home on the site. Architects believe that the original brick structure built by Mr. Bent was incorporated into the "new" fourteen-room mansion that was constructed by Seth Ward in 1871. The home is located just east of Ward Parkway (named after Hugh Ward), which passes near the Seth E. Ward Home. The home is listed in the National Register of Historic Places, and a sign was placed on the property by the Westport Historical Society. Today, the home remains a private residence.

Read More

Airway Pioneers: Richard Flying Field, by Lois Allen and Roberta Bonnewitz
Back in Independence, by Mary Paxton Keeley
The Bidwell-Bartleson Party 1851 California Emigrant Adventure, by Dr. Doyce B. Nunis Jr.
Brief History of Fort Leavenworth, by John W. Partin
A Century of Kansas City Aviation, by George R. Bauer
Independence (Images of America), by Richard N. Piland and Marietta Wilson Boenker
Kansas City's Parks and Boulevards (Images of America), by Patrick Alley and Dona Boley
Leavenworth, *Fort Leavenworth* and *U.S. Penitentiary Leavenworth* (Images of America), each by Kenneth M. LaMaster
Memories of Weston, Missouri, by Sandra Lewis Miller
Missouri Star: The Life and Times of Martha A. "Mattie" (Livingston) Lykins Bingham, by Rose Ann Findlen
Mountain Man James Bridger: The "Daniel Boone of the Rocky Mountains," by William S. Brackett

Mount Washington and the Shaping of Kansas City, by Bruce Matthews
On Slavery's Border: Missouri's Small Slaveholding Households, 1815–1865, by Diane Mutti Burke
Path to Glory: A Pictorial Celebration of the Santa Fe Trail, by Jami Parkinson
Raytown Remembers, by Roberta Bonnewitz
Raytown, Missouri, USA, by Raytown Historical Society
Santa Fe Trail National Historic Trail Comprehensive Management and Use Plan, by the National Park Service
Scattered to the Four Winds: General Order No. 11 and Martial Law in Jackson County, Missouri, 1863, by Ralph Monaco II
Survivors: A Catalog of Missouri's Remaining 19th Century County Courthouses, by J. Bradley Pace
Treasure in a Cornfield: The Discovery and Excavation of the Steamboat Arabia, by Greg Hawley
Winding the Clock on the Independence Square: Jackson County's Historic Truman Courthouse, by David W. Jackson

3

BUILDERS AND DREAMERS

Kansas City was more than just a stop on the way west; it was the last stop on the Missouri River Route, and it was the first stop of many thousand-mile journeys. The Santa Fe, California, and Oregon Trails all spread out from and fed into Kansas City. Trade with Mexico (which had gained its independence from Spain in 1821) brought great opportunities to Missouri and built the fortunes of traders on both ends of the trail. Speculators, town-builders and conmen, as well as priests, missionaries and prostitutes, all found their way to the area. Traders and suppliers in the West found customers in the Native American tribes, who received annual payments from the U.S. government; their Mexican counterparts in Santa Fe; French fur trappers; and settlers who were heading out on the Oregon and California Trails.

After the 1826 flood, Chouteau's community moved to the south bank of the Missouri River, and the town that would become Kansas City grew up there. Today's City Market encompasses the area the French resettled and has been in continuous operation, in one form or another, since 1857. The community in what was then known as the French Bottoms received a priest as early as 1836, and the first log cabin church was built by Father Roux (with the financial support and involvement of Berenice Chouteau). The land purchased by Father Roux has been home to a series of Catholic churches ever since; currently, it is the site of the Cathedral of the Immaculate Conception between Eleventh and Twelfth Streets, on Broadway Boulevard. In the 1850s, Father Bernard Donnelley brought in three hundred Irish workmen from Connaught, Ireland, to lay the bricks of the St. Francis Regis

Church. Completed in 1857, the old brick building is now the chapel of the Cathedral of the Immaculate Conception. Many of the workmen who were brought in by Father Donnelley stayed in the town to help dig out the roads that led up the bluffs from the river. Together, they formed the core of the area's Irish Catholic community.

Though commerce, adventure and the chance to own land brought many to the area, the allure of the West also drew the attention of reformers and missionaries of every kind. Circuit-riding Methodist preachers visited the remote corners of the territory to spread the gospel, and by 1835, Westport United Methodist Church was established. There were also many early Baptist churches in the area, including Six Mile Baptist Church (1825) of Sibley and First Baptist of Kansas City. Presbyterian congregations were also built in Independence and Westport in 1836.

In 1831, members of the Mormon Church flocked to the Kansas City area, and some made efforts to convert the newly arrived Native Americans to Mormonism. Then, the church's founder, Joseph Smith, told his followers that Independence, Missouri, had been chosen as the location of their temple. Conflicts between the earlier settlers and the Mormons—over religion, politics and financial competition—hit a boiling point, and they soon turned ugly, as the newcomers were forcibly driven from Independence, Jackson County and, later, Missouri altogether. The Mormon town of Far West (about fifty-five miles northeast of Kansas City) had a population of three thousand in 1838, but the entire community was forced to flee by the Missouri volunteer militia, which was under the command of Governor Lilburn Boggs. Many historic sites related to this early Mormon history remain in the Kansas City area, including the Historic Liberty Jail in Liberty, where Joseph Smith and other Mormon Church leaders were imprisoned; the Temple Lot; the old Stone Church; and several other sites in Independence and other nearby communities. Today, the Mormon Church and several of its branches maintain a presence throughout the city.

The first synagogue in Kansas City, Bnai Jehudah, was established in 1870, although there had been a number of Jewish traders and settlers in town since the late 1830s. The various communities of faith in Kansas City shaped the city's growth. They added churches, cemeteries and schools to the landscape, and they often (but not always) led the charge toward social reform for the betterment of the greater community.

The 1840s saw explosive growth and change in the communities along the Santa Fe and Oregon Trails. Many travelers followed the traditional route and jumped off at Independence, where they could find all the necessities for a long trip. There were springs all around the town, and travelers were able to stock up on drinking water before beginning their arduous journeys across the prairie. But there were other jumping-off points on the Missouri River, and every potential landing point seemed to have a town growing up around it.

St. Joseph, Missouri, is about sixty miles north of Kansas City, and, like Independence, it was a competitor of Kansas City during its early days. Founded by fur trader Joseph Robidoux, and incorporated in 1843, St. Joseph was a popular starting point for the Oregon and, later, California Trails. It had a busy port, and it became the starting point of the Pony Express; it also had railroad connections to the East well before Kansas City. Today, the lines between these neighboring communities blur more every year, as they grow closer together, and their competition and interaction had a great impact on the metropolitan center that Kansas City has become.

Alexander Majors was an enterprising farmer who parlayed his knowledge of horses and oxen into a wildly successful business. He made a fortune in freight hauling and organizing wagon trains; he also cofounded several business ventures, including the Pony Express. His property was located on what was then a little path that extended down from the city, to the Santa Fe Trail; today, that trail is known as State Line Road. In 1848, on his first freight hauling jaunt down the Santa Fe Trail, Majors set a record pace of ninety-two days for the over 1,500-mile round trip. Within a few years, he employed thousands of drivers and teams. In 1853, Majors received military contracts to haul supplies to the forts on the Santa Fe Trail. In 1854, he partnered with William B. Waddell and William Hepburn Russell to start the Major's & Russell Freight Hauling Firm (Waddell's name was added later). While Majors took a hands-on approach to the freight hauling business, Waddell managed the office and Russell focused on using his Washington, D.C., contacts to acquire new contracts for the firm.

The trio brought so much business to the area that Majors is credited as one of the founding fathers of Kansas City and is depicted as such at Pioneer Park, at the juncture of Broadway and Westport Roads, with the sculpture *The Pioneers*. Majors's mark remains all over the Kansas City area. In Westport, he set up a meat-packing plant that also supplied his wagon trains with cured pork, soap and candles. In Kansas City, he had a warehouse that stored the many supplies his wagons used. In St. Joseph, the Pony Express is memorialized in a museum. The stockyards in the West Bottoms were built on land that he had purchased for his freight company. His home at the

Alexander Majors's house, 8145 State Line, Kansas City, Missouri. *Courtesy of the Library of Congress Prints and Photographs Division (MO HABS MO,48-KANCI,5—1).*

corner of Eighty-First Street and State Line Road was built in 1856; today, it is maintained by the Wornall-Majors House Museums.

In 1857, James B. and Lucinda Mahaffie moved to the newly formed town of Olathe, Kansas (now the fourth-largest city in the state). The next year, the Mahaffies hauled their wood-frame home from its downtown lot to a plot of land they purchased about a mile outside of town. The family lived in that home until a new stone house, which still stands, was built in 1865. The family was already hosting travelers from the trails as early as 1858, but in 1864, the Barlow, Sanderson and Company Stagecoach Line contracted with the Mahaffie family to provide one of the stops the company needed for its coaches carrying passengers and mail between Fort Scott and Fort Leavenworth (or west on the route to Santa Fe). From 1865 until around 1870, coach passengers and other hungry travelers ate their meals in the basement of the "new" stone farmhouse. In those days, the Mahaffies may have served as many as one hundred meals per day. As the stage lines faded away with the arrival of the railroads, the Mahaffie farm continued to prosper, and a series of families kept the business going after the Mahaffies retired and moved back into town. The farm and stagecoach stop are now popular stops for locals and tourists alike. The community that the trails and trains left behind became one of the city's more popular suburbs, when the post–World War II era put it back on the map with the arrival of Interstate 35.

A mill commonly known as the Watts Mill (first known as Fitzhugh's Mill) once stood on the north bank of Indian Creek. This mill was built in 1832 by Jackson County judge John Fitzhugh, who operated it as a sawmill. The Santa Fe Trail passed nearby, and travelers often used the site as a campground; when it became a gristmill, travelers used it to stock up on corn meal and flour. Since it was close to the Kansas-Missouri border, both Native Americans and settlers brought their grain to the mill, leaving one-fifth of the grist as payment. The mill changed hands a few times, and was even owned by Daniel Boone's grandson Albert G. Boone at one point. In 1850, Anthony Watts purchased the mill, and it continued to operate as the Watts family business until Anthony's son, Stubbins Watts, passed away in 1922.

In 1838, John Calvin McCoy and several other local businessmen formed the Town of Kansas Company, which purchased the estate of Gabriel Prudhomme. McCoy had set up a dock at a rocky point in the river, between Main Street and Grand Boulevard, but Prudhomme's farm comprised all of the present-day River Market area around it. The property was purchased by the Town of Kansas Company, but litigation over the sale and between members of the group lasted until 1846. Town of Kansas Company was looking forward to building up the area and set land aside between Fourth and Fifth Streets and Walnut and Main Streets, for a public square. Its timing was fortunate, as a number of events contributed greatly to the development of the city's economy. The admission of Texas to the Union; the 1846 Oregon Treaty with Britain, which added the Washington and Oregon Territories to the western United States; and the war with Mexico, which ended in the annexation of California and the southwest territories, all created new markets and destinations for goods passing from Kansas City's river route to the trails.

The discovery of gold in the California Territory, coupled with the promise of land in Oregon, turned the nation's trek west into a race, and the City Market was flooded with families who were hoping to settle in the new territories, and Forty-Niners, who had gold fever and were in need of supplies. The Kansas-Nebraska Act of 1854 added even more territory to the nation, and it introduced a new kind of immigrant, as antislavery groups sent settlers

City market, Kansas City, Missouri. *Courtesy of the Library of Congress Prints and Photographs Division (LC-D401-19219; LC-DIG-det-4a13237).*

to Kansas to make it a free state. In 1857, the city leased land on the west end of the market to the Scheibel Brothers, who built the first market building. The town dug streets up through the bluffs and eventually financed the leveling of the impediments to growth through bonds issued in the 1850s.

In 1888, the city built a brick market building on Walnut Street, near Fifth Street, with fifty-six stalls, but the market soon outgrew that facility. In 1910, the city purchased land between Third and Fourth Streets, doubling the size of the market. The city added cable cars to its transportation system in the 1880s, and in 1900, it added street cars that connected the City Market to the growing city, reducing wagon traffic (although vendors continued to bring produce to the market in horse-drawn wagons well into the early twentieth century). The blocks near City Market became a busy hub of illegal activity; the section of Main Street across from city hall and police headquarters even became known as Battle Row. There were dozens of gambling dens and bawdy houses within a short walk of the City Market, where the nameless cowboys and river rats mingled with the likes of Wild Bill Hickok and Wyatt Earp.

CHOUTEAU'S CHURCH, ST. FRANCIS REGIS AND CATHEDRAL OF THE IMMACULATE CONCEPTION

416 West Twelfth Street
Kansas City, Missouri 64105
816-842-0416
www.kcgolddome.org

The first Catholic church in the Kansas City area was a log structure built in 1835 on land purchased by Father Benedict Roux. Saint John Francis Regis Church served the tiny community and its many settlers for a number of years. Although it has been replaced, restored and renamed over the years, there has been a Catholic church on that piece of land ever since. The Cathedral of the Immaculate Conception, with its iconic gold leaf–covered dome and cross that soars 250 feet above the street, was the tallest building in Kansas City when it began holding services in 1883. It still serves as a landmark and is a contributing property in the Quality Hill neighborhood, which is listed in the National Register of Historic Places. Tours of the church are available, and a marker commemorating its history is located on the corner of Eleventh and Washington Streets.

UPPER INDEPENDENCE LANDING AND WAYNE CITY OVERLOOK

1533–2219 Wayne City Road
Sugar Creek, Missouri 64050
www.3trailscorridor.com/waypoints/wayne-city-landing

Wayne City Landing served as a port that received supplies for early pioneers and goods that were heading to Santa Fe in Mexico and, later, the Oregon Territory. Wayne City is listed in the National Register of Historic Places, as it was one of the early starting points of the trails heading west. The first railroad west of the Mississippi River was built in Wayne City and was used to haul goods from the river to nearby Independence. South of the town, there is an overlook with a short trail, benches, and several interpretive signs above the landing and a big rock that visitors can climb on to get a good view of the Missouri River Valley. River Boulevard leads directly to Independence Square from the landing and, in the past, would have passed by the homestead of Samuel Combs Owens, a prominent Santa Fe Trail merchant and one of the incorporators of the Town of Kansas (discussed elsewhere in this book). The house was passed on to William McCoy, who became the first mayor of the newly incorporated City of Independence. Information on the house can be found at www.owensmccoyhouse.com.

ALEXANDER MAJORS HOUSE MUSEUM

8201 State Line Road
Kansas City, Missouri 64114
816-444-1858
www.wornallmajors.org

The Alexander Majors House was built in 1856, and it is listed in the National Register of Historic Places. It was the home and headquarters of Alexander Majors and his freighting operation. Majors employed thousands of men and used thousands of wagons and horses to haul freight to military outposts on the Santa Fe Trail, people to the western territories and mail and other freight to private businesses along the way. The house faces west; there, Majors could look across the state line and see land he leased in Kansas, which was filled with livestock and busy with blacksmiths and wagon masters preparing for the trails. The successful businessman may have also leased this land because property in the Kansas Territory couldn't be taxed by the local or state government in Missouri. The house has authentic period furnishings and artifacts that are related to Major's life. The museum also has both tour-guided and self-guided tours available.

FITZHUGH-WATT'S MILL

103rd Street and Wornall Road
Kansas City, Missouri
www.newsantafe.org/mill

Built in 1832 by Judge John Fitzhugh, this mill on Indian Creek became a popular stop along the Santa Fe Trail. It changed hands several times before it was purchased by Anthony Watts, whose family kept it operating until 1922. In 1942, Edgar Watts, Anthony Watt's grandson, scrapped the abandoned mill and contributed the metal from its machinery to aid the war effort during World War II. A marker was erected at the site by the Native Sons and Daughters of Kansas City; it shows where the mill once stood and is set next to one of the original mill stones. Parts of the mill's original limestone foundation can still be seen along the banks of Indian Creek, and the paved Indian Creek Greenway Trail passes through the park, which is located near popular restaurants and shopping areas.

CITY MARKET

Fifth and Walnut Streets
Kansas City, Missouri 64106
816-842-127
www.thecitymarket.org

The historic river market, or City Market, has been open for business for nearly 180 years. Built up from the landing east of the intersection of the Kansas and Missouri Rivers, the open-air market and its shops and restaurants provide visitors the opportunity to shop, sample and explore the oldest section of Kansas City. In addition to the market's over forty permanent shops, specialty grocers and market vendors, its popular Steamboat *Arabia* Museum serves as an attraction to history lovers.

KANSAS CITY IRISH CENTER

15 West Linwood Boulevard
Kansas City, Missouri 64111
816-474-3848
www.irishcenterkc.org

Organized with the mission "to celebrate, support, preserve and promote Irish heritage and culture," the Kansas City Irish Center initially opened on St. Patrick's Day 2007, at Union Station. The site was appropriate considering how many Irish laborers had been involved in building the railroads that fed into the busy hub. By 2016, the Kansas City Irish Center had outgrown the station, so it purchased the historic Drexel Hall, a building at the corner of

Linwood Boulevard and Baltimore Avenue. The new location is closer to Kansas City's historic Irish neighborhoods and has become an important partner in many of the Irish events that are held in Kansas City.

MORMON VISITORS CENTER

937 West Walnut Street
Independence, Missouri 64050
816-836-3466

COMMUNITY OF CHRIST INTERNATIONAL HEADQUARTERS

1001 West Walnut Street
Independence, Missouri 64050
816-833-1000

Independence Square, the temple lot, the temple and the auditorium are central locations in the history of the Mormon Church. The Mormon visitors' center has exhibits that depict the experiences of settlers from the early days of the faith and is a good starting point for anyone wanting to explore the history of Mormons in Missouri. The Community of Christ Stone Church and the enormous temple, as well as several other historical sites, are all within walking distance of the visitors' center.

HISTORIC LIBERTY JAIL

216 North Main Street
Liberty, Missouri 64068
816-781-3188

The old Liberty Jail, in Liberty, Missouri, is where Joseph Smith, founder of the Latter-day Saint movement, and his associates were imprisoned for four months during the 1838 Mormon War. Joseph Smith received revelations during his imprisonment there, and the site is now owned by the Church of Jesus Christ of Latter-day Saints (LDS Church), which operates a visitors' center there that displays an indoor, cutaway reconstruction of the old jail.

MAHAFFIE STAGECOACH STOP AND FARM

1200 East Kansas City Road
Olathe, Kansas 66061
913-971-5111
www.mahaffie.org

In the 1860s, the Mahaffie Farm was a way station for travelers on the Barlow, Sanderson and Company Stagecoach Line, and it served as a family farm. Today, the Mahaffie Historic Site is operated by the City of Olathe's Parks and Recreation Department. The site has also been dedicated as an official component of the Santa Fe National Historic Trail by the National Park Service, and it is a partner site of Freedom's Frontier National Heritage Area. Visitors can enjoy a variety of experiences from riding in one of the stagecoaches to exploring the farm, home and outbuildings. The site also contains a blacksmith shop, a large horse and oxen barn with exhibits, a corral, a chicken coop, a wash house, a peg barn, an ice house, a smoke house, the farm home, a cellar, farm implements, livestock, planted fields and a heritage center with more exhibits.

MISSOURI TOWN 1855 (FLEMING PARK)

8010 East Park Road
Lee's Summit, Missouri 64064
816-524-8770
www.makeyourdayhere.com/MissouriTown

Missouri Town 1855 is a living history museum comprising more than twenty-five buildings that date from 1820 to 1860. Representing the nineteenth-century lifestyle of a small farming community, the park employs interpreters in period attire to grow authentic field and garden crops and to raise rare livestock breeds. The museum is located in Fleming Park, which is part of the Jackson County, Missouri park system.

NATIONAL FRONTIER TRAILS MUSEUM

318 West Pacific Avenue
Independence, Missouri 64050
816-325-7575
www.ci.independence.mo.us/nftm

Located in the primary "jumping off" town of Independence, Missouri, the Merrill J. Mattes Research Library at the National Frontier Trails Museum is a public research library focused on the overland trails and the acquisition and settlement of the American West. It is the largest public research library in the nation devoted to the western trails. Its collection contains over 2,600 first-person trail accounts, authentic covered wagons, trail artifacts, original diaries and letters. Its exhibits include an interactive "Pack Your Wagon with the Campbells," a hands-on experience in which children learn how to pack a wagon for the trail. A spring that was once used by the pioneers is located on the site, and wagon ruts or "swales" are still visible on the property after nearly two hundred years.

National Frontier Trails Museum, 318 West Pacific Avenue, Independence, Missouri. *Courtesy of Paul Kirkman.*

Read More

Direct Your Letters to San Jose: The California Gold Rush Letters and Diary of James and David Lee Campbell, 1849–1852, by David W. Jackson

Early Independence, Missouri: Mormon History Tour Guide, by Ronald E. Romig

From the Bottom Up: The Story of the Irish in Kansas City, by Pat O'Neill

The LDS Family Travel Guide: Independence to Nauvoo, by Becky Cardon Smith

Liberty Jail and the Legacy of Joseph, by Thomas D. Cottle

Merchants of Independence: International Trade on the Santa Fe Trail, 1827–1860, by William Patrick O'Brien

Missouri Town-1855: A Program in Architectural Preservation, by LaVonne Belew Moore

Seventy Years on the Frontier: Alexander Majors' Memoirs (or, *A Lifetime on the Border*), by Alexander Majors

This Far by Faith: A Popular History of the Catholic People of West and Northwest Missouri, by Dorothy Brandt Marra, Colette Doering, Bill R. Beemont and Michael Coleman

4

BLEEDING KANSAS (CITY)

The same forces that created a thriving city at the edge of the western frontier nearly destroyed it in the mid-nineteenth century. The acquisition of new territories in the West, coupled with improved communication and travel through railroad and telegraph connections, Kansas City was poised to be a central hub, connecting the East and the West. In the 1850s, however, the only things that seemed to matter were North and South.

As territories vied to become states, the balance of power between the slave-holding Southern states and the free Northern states was upended. The war of words in the East escalated into a war of guns and cannons on the western frontier. The older settlements in Missouri had grown out of a slave economy, and there was a presumption that this way of life would naturally expand into the nearby Kansas Territory. But when Congress passed the Kansas-Nebraska Act in 1854, the territories themselves were left to decide whether they would be free or slave states.

Beginning in 1854, Kansas was besieged with competing legislatures, constitutions and governors. When the first vote was taken to decide whether Kansas would be a free or slave state, large numbers of Missourians crossed the border and skewed the election by casting illegal ballots, threatening free-state voters and chasing them from the polls at gunpoint. The violence between the free-state and proslavery forces led to the 1856 Sacking of Lawrence, in which proslavery forces burned down the Free-State Hotel, destroyed newspaper offices and looted the town of Lawrence, Kansas. When the smoke cleared, the reaction back East resulted in a brawl in Congress,

John Brown. *Courtesy of the Library of Congress Prints and Photographs Division (LC-DIG-ppmsca-23763).*

a three-way split in the Democrat Party and howls at the injustice of Missourians crossing the border and sullying the vote. Kansas City soon found itself awash in new traffic heading for the Kansas Territory. Proslavery settlers crossed into the territory, and Immigrant Aid Societies sprang up across the North, hoping to out-populate and out-vote the proslavery settlers. Towns like Lawrence (named after Amos Adams Lawrence, the treasurer of the New England Emigrant Aid Society) grew up to counter proslavery towns, like Atchison and Leavenworth.

Among the early settlers in the Kansas Territory who were enraged by the actions of the proslavery forces was John Brown. His sons had moved to the territory and wrote back that they feared for their lives. In response, Brown moved to Kansas in the autumn of 1855 and took part in several armed actions in 1856. He murdered a group of proslavery settlers in Potowatomi, and one of his sons was killed by proslavery raiders in an attack on Ossawatomie. Brown's experiences led him to the conclusion that a violent overthrow of the slave owners was the only way to end slavery. Abolitionists who were out to actually free slaves took part in the Underground Railroad and used the port at Quindaro, Kansas, which had been set up in 1857 to transport runaway and liberated slaves to freedom.

From 1857 to 1858, the official capital of the Kansas Territory was Lecompton. Constitution Hall, where a proslavery legislature voted for a proslavery constitution in 1857, still stands. This proslavery constitution was the second of four constitutions that were sent by four different legislatures from four different capitals in Kansas. The Lecompton constitution was a major topic in the Lincoln-Douglas debates and was ultimately rejected by Congress, as were the Topeka and Leavenworth constitutions. The fourth and final of Kansas's constitutions was sent to Congress and signed in Wyandotte (now Kansas City, Kansas), in a hall over a warehouse north of Kaw Point. This constitution languished in the Democrat-dominated Congress until after Lincoln was elected.

Constitution Hall, 315 Elmore Street, Lecompton, Douglas County, Kansas. *Courtesy of the Library of Congress Prints and Photographs Division (HABS KANS,23-LECOM,1—1).*

The bloody conflict in Kansas presaged the Civil War, and it bitterly divided the many communities that made up the Kansas City area. Though the headlines were dominated by the nation's fierce struggle over slavery, the city's business community continued to press for expansion, lobby for railroad service and seek government contracts. The Pony Express, was founded by William H. Russell, William B. Waddell and Alexander Majors. Russell was the driving force behind the business, but there was a genuine need for its services at the time. The Butterfield Overland Stage Line had previously carried mail to the West, but its routes went south, through Texas, and as the specter of secession and war loomed, an alternate route for communication was needed between the East and the new western territories. None of the railroads had reached Kansas City yet, but north of the Missouri River, rail service had made its way to St. Joseph.

The Pony Express had more than one hundred stations, eighty riders and between four hundred and five hundred horses. The men rode short distances, at break-neck speeds, through dangerous territory; they ran relays, with saddle bags filled with mail, over a two-thousand-mile course. The Pony Express's service began in April 1860, as riders left simultaneously from St. Joseph, Missouri, and Sacramento, California. The trek took between ten and twelve days, averaging over two hundred miles a day. Lincoln's inaugural address was carried by the riders at a record pace, and the trip took just eight days. The riders only lost one bag of mail during the nineteen months the route was in service. Only six riders were lost, but sixteen of the isolated station stockmen were killed. Two days after the telegraph service to California was established, the Pony Express went out of business. But the memories of the bold riders galloping through the wilderness were kept alive by the people who had seen them firsthand: Mark Twain, Frederic Remington and "Buffalo Bill" Cody. Cody even performed reenactments of the Pony Express in his Wild West Shows, which toured the United States and Europe and were seen by millions over the course of thirty years. The Pony Express Museum in St. Joseph keeps the story of the Pony Express alive and is one of several must-sees in Kansas City.

By 1860, Kansas City's many communities were as divided over slavery as any place in America. The long and often bloody Border War had culminated in the Kansas Territory electing to be a free state. The state's legislature then approved a constitution and applied for statehood in 1859. Kansas's leading citizens, men of wealth and power who had helped build their communities, were soon forced to take a position and take up arms to defend it, as neutrality became untenable. Men in the Kansas City area, like Dr. Johnston Lykins and former Kansas City mayor William S. Gregory, had kinship ties and roots in the South. Lykin's wife was forced to leave the city, and Gregory also left the city for the duration of the war.

Many of Independence and Kansas City's leading citizens were also slave-owners. Slavery in Missouri was legal, common and profitable. Many of these men were unwilling to consider accepting the financial ruin that abolition could have had on the state's economy; their personal wealth and livelihoods

Pony Express Museum, St. Joseph, Missouri. *Courtesy of the Library of Congress Prints and Photographs Division (HABS MO, -SAJOE,16—11).*

were tied to the institution of slavery. Even those who didn't own slaves were often tied financially and personally to those who did. Kansas City bankers, lawyers and businessmen also had slaves in their homes and their businesses, as well as on their farms. The largest slave owner in the state of Missouri, Jabez Smith, lived in Independence. Everyone, from Reverend Thomas Johnson to John Calvin McCoy, had slaves, yet, many staunch antislavery advocates were also counted among the city's elites, including businessmen and town promoters like Kersey Coates and Robert T. Van Horn. Coates was originally from Pennsylvania, and on Election Day 1860, he organized a militia to protect and escort the few voters who favored Lincoln to the polls. Van Horn was a lawyer who also grew up in Pennsylvania; he owned the *Kansas City Journal* newspaper and served as the mayor of Kansas City during much of the Civil War; he also served as a lieutenant colonel in the Union army.

In some parts of Kansas City, a slave could be working in a field just a few hundred feet from the state line—and freedom. When the Civil War broke out, many slaves escaped by running across the border. Some joined the Union army and served in Kansas militia units, praying for the day when their families and fellow slaves would be free. A few even joined the Confederate army or guerrilla units; they were angered by the depredations of the Kansas Jayhawkers and Red Legs, who frequently burned and looted the slave quarters alongside the plantation homes, destroying the communities that they had grown up in.

Native Americans were divided during the Civil War, too; some owned slaves and others joined the Union cause. Many Native Americans in the Kansas City area owned land and had intermarried with white settlers. They were caught in the middle and pushed to prove their loyalty by joining the Union forces. The decision to fight with the South would have meant that old treaties could be nullified. But standing against the Southerners could have meant reprisals and attacks by the guerrillas. Several tribes split on the issue, and there were Native American units involved in the fighting in Texas, Arkansas, Oklahoma (then called the Indian Territory) and Southwest Missouri.

The 1860 presidential election saw Missouri splitting its vote, with Northern Democrat Stephen Douglas edging out Constitutional Union Party candidate John Bell; Abraham Lincoln placed at a distant fourth, behind the Southern Democratic Party contender John C. Breckenridge. While most Missourians didn't favor secession, there were many who hoped to remain neutral and avoid conflict with their neighbors and family members from other states. Missouri's governorship went to Democrat Claiborne Fox Jackson, who had misrepresented himself as a neutral who was against secession. Kansas City watched helplessly as Missouri devolved into two armed camps, with federal troops literally chasing the governor and legislature from the capitol and armies and militias battling throughout the state. The bonds that had held the community together were destroyed, as militias, guerrillas and commissioned troops from both sides of the conflict became embroiled in an escalating and personal war that was far from civil.

On the Kansas side of the state line, militiamen led by Senator James Lane and Charles "Doc" Jennison were based in Lawrence and Westport, respectively. After gaining initial victories at Wilson's Creek and Lexington, the Missouri State Guard, led by former governor Sterling Price, was outnumbered by the Union forces and was forced to hurriedly withdraw. The Guardsmen left many of the men who fought at Lexington behind, as they could not feed them or provide them with horses. Reeling from the loss at the Battle of Pea Ridge, the governor, Missouri State Guard and much of the elected legislature left the state. Since Missouri's bid to secede was rejected as invalid by the Union (although the state received a star on the rebel flag and representation in the Confederate congress), any members of the Missouri State Guard who failed to surrender and join the Union forces were considered guerrillas—criminals who could be killed outright. As these Missouri soldiers were being transported east to fight against the Confederate armies, they realized that if they joined the fight, they would likely be facing family members and friends on the battlefield.

The young men from the Kansas City area who had volunteered to join Price's Confederate army but did not want to abandon their homes and families to march to Arkansas joined guerrilla outfits—like those of William Quantrill and "Bloody" Bill Anderson. Frank and Jesse James, whose father was a college-educated minister, and Cole Younger, whose father was a very successful businessman and Missouri state senator, were among the many teenagers in the area who threw in their lot with the ill-fated guerrilla leaders.

With the advent of Civil War, the Kansas-Missouri border was set ablaze. Slave-freeing raids, which were carried out by groups of Kansans, became punitive expeditions to get back at the Missourians who had done so much damage to Kansas communities. Whole towns were looted and burned on the Missouri side, and livestock and property were often "liberated," whether or not the Missouri families owned slaves. Reprisal attacks from Missouri bushwhackers also devolved into the sacking and burning of farms and communities on the Kansas side of the border. As the fighting continued, the states' populations moved; individuals and entire towns also switched their alliances. The town of Atchison had been named after Missouri senator David Rice Atchison and had been settled by individuals from the proslavery faction in the 1850s. Frustrated federal commanders in Missouri saw trains derailed, stagecoaches carrying mail attacked, bridges burned, telegraph wires cut and towns robbed and raided by these wild young men (both Anderson and Quantrill were in their early twenties at the start of the war). Quantrill attacked Olathe and Shawnee in Kansas, and Jennison and Lane attacked Rose Hill and Osceola in Missouri—back and forth the attacks went.

In 1861, Senator Lane scorched the Kansas-Missouri border and was infamously quoted as saying that he wanted to clear Missouri of "everything disloyal from a Shanghai rooster to a Durham cow." The Rebels found shelter and help in the proslavery towns of Missouri, and a series of attempts to deny the Rebels shelter led to the most notorious and heinous acts that occurred on either side of the border. In 1862, Confederate forces, aided by Quantrill's guerrillas, attacked Independence, killing more than three hundred Union troops and forcing the remaining men to surrender. The next week, the Confederates gained another victory at the Battle of Lone Jack.

Concern over guerrillas' continued successes led to the issuance of Order No. 10 by Union commander Major General Samuel Curtis; this order gave the federal troops the ability to round up the female family members of known and suspected guerrillas and jail them until they could be deported from the state. In August 1863, a group of women was held under this order at 1425 Grand Avenue (today's Sprint Arena is in this location) in Kansas City. The building they were being held in collapsed on August 13, 1863 (many believed the building was either purposely weakened or knowingly neglected), killing four women, including the fifteen-year-old sister of Bill Anderson. Anderson's ten-year-old sister was also in the building, chained to a bed, and was horribly and permanently crippled by the collapse. William Quantrill had already been planning a raid on Lawrence, Kansas, but after the jail collapse, Anderson and his men were hell-bent on revenge and joined forces with Quantrill. Lawrence's doom was sealed.

A week after the jail collapse, the guerrillas slipped across the state line, and, on the morning of August 21, 1863, they rode into the town and attacked, killing 150 men and teenage boys and looting and burning most of the town's business district and several targeted residences. Senator Lane hid in a field during the raid, and Colonel Jennison was out of town. The shock and anger at the raid led many Kansans to clamor for a punitive attack on the citizens of Missouri. But most Missourians still supported the Union, and the state had supplied over 100,000 men to the Union cause, nearly three times the number that the state had supplied to the Confederacy.

The Union army believed Quantrill's guerrillas drew their support from the rural population of the four Missouri counties on the Kansas border, south of the Missouri River: Bates, Cass, Jackson and part of Vernon. Following the sacking of Lawrence, federal forces were determined to end such raiding and insurgency by any means necessary—no matter what the cost might be to innocent civilians. General Thomas Ewing, who had lost several lifelong friends in the raid, issued Order No. 11. Ewing's decree (issued just four days after the August 21 massacre) enacted martial law on the Union's own citizens for the first time in American history. It ordered the expulsion of all residents from these counties, except for those living within one mile of the town limits of Independence, Hickman Mills, Pleasant Hill and Harrisonville. The area of Kansas City, Missouri, north of Brush Creek and west of the Big Blue River, was also spared. When Ewing signed Order No. 11, he forced thousands of Missourians in four counties (mostly women, children and the elderly) to pack up whatever belongings they could and leave their homes with only fifteen days' notice. Kansas Jayhawkers and Red Legs came across the border to enforce the rule and left with wagonloads of the produce and personal belongings of the over twenty thousand Missourians

Depiction of William Clarke Quantrill's retaliation on Lawrence, Kansas, August 21, 1863. *Courtesy of the Library of Congress Prints and Photographs Division (LC-USZ62-134452).*

who were affected by the order. Among those who were displaced were Harry Truman's mother, the James brothers' family, the Dalton brothers' family, the Youngers and a young Carrie Nation.

By the end of the Civil War, the leaders of the proslavery faction had completely changed their tune. Firebrand planter and slave owner Benjamin Franklin Stringfellow, who had led troops in the sacking of Lawrence, struck Kansas territorial governor Andrew Reeder with a chair and promoted and participated in voter fraud in Kansas. Stringfellow ended up being a Republican investor and attorney for the Atchison, Topeka & Santa Fe Railroad.

The post–Civil War outlaw era; the class resentment of the elites, whose roles had been reversed; the despair and will of survivors to reform; and the eventual resurgence of the Democratic Party in the Kansas City area all have their beginnings in this series of escalating events. Artist George Caleb Bingham was so aghast at the depredations set in motion by General Ewing that he created a painting memorializing the infamous order. Years after the war, when Ewing ran for governor in Ohio, Bingham's son toured the state with copies of the work, titled *Order No. 11* or *Martial Law*, in a successful effort to contribute to Ewing's defeat.

By the late summer of 1864, the population of western Missouri had been greatly depleted. Burned-out and abandoned homes stretched out along both sides of the Kansas-Missouri border. Trail traffic and construction in Kansas City had been greatly diminished, and the upcoming national election was overshadowed by the horrible results of the Battles of Vicksburg and Gettysburg—as the loss of so many American lives seemed to foreshadow another year of warfare.

A desperate and doomed plan to ignite a second front and knock Kansas and Missouri out of the election (and perhaps advance former general and presidential candidate George McClellan over Abraham Lincoln in the process) was undertaken by General Sterling Price. The invasion of Missouri ultimately led all military forces to the communities near the Missouri River's bend, where the largest Civil War battle west of the Mississippi took place.

Price entered Missouri in September, hoping to take the arsenal in St. Louis or the capitol in Jefferson City and draw Union forces away from the fight in Georgia. He also argued that he could get thousands of recruits from Missouri and bring back horses, cattle and supplies from the raid. But Price moved too slowly, and he gave the federal forces time to reinforce both towns; he was forced to turn west across the state. Communications were poor, but word eventually came that his army was working its way toward

Kansas. After picking up uniforms and equipment in Glasgow and Sedalia and over one thousand recruits in Boonville, Price continued to advance.

Major General James G. Blunt had left Independence with a force of two thousand men to find Price (the guerrillas had cut telegraph wires and left the city isolated from news of Price's whereabouts). Blunt engaged with Price's forces at Lexington (forty miles from Kansas City), but he was greatly outnumbered and retreated toward Independence. At the Little Blue River, Blunt saw a perfect spot to trap Price. He left a small force of four hundred men, under the command of Colonel Thomas Moonlight, at the crossing, hoping to convince Major General Samuel Curtis to send enough troops to trap Price in the valley before he got to Independence and Kansas City. However, the Kansas militias were unwilling to cross into Missouri, past the Big Blue River; Curtis was focused on stopping Price at the state line. Blunt returned to the Little Blue River on the morning of October 21, 1864, and he found that Moonlight's little force had been fighting Price's force of several thousand men since dawn. Blunt had nine hundred men with him, but they were still vastly outnumbered. Blunt fought a delaying action against Price that lasted all day and dragged through Independence.

The next day, the Confederates feinted toward Kansas City and worked their way south, along the Big Blue River, until they found a crossing through which they could force their way. At Byram's Ford, the Confederates drove the Kansas militia back to the state line, north of Brush Creek, but the Battle of the Little Blue had cost them a day that they couldn't afford.

Battle of the Little Blue Civil War, marker placed by Civil War Round Table of Western Missouri. *Courtesy of Paul Kirkman.*

Colonel Alfred Pleasanton had been pursuing Price with a veteran cavalry force of over four thousand men. While Price's forces pushed across the Big Blue River at Byram's Ford, Pleasanton was driving his rearguard out of Independence. The citizens of Independence witnessed two fierce battles, with thousands of men, back-to-back in the streets of their town. The Confederate retreat and Pleasonton's advance, which took place on the opposite ends of town, could be seen from the second floor of the Bingham-Waggoner Home.

On the morning of October 23, 1864, Price entered the field with fewer than ten thousand men against a combined federal force of more than twenty thousand men. He had hoped to defeat Curtis—maybe turn north, toward Kansas City or Leavenworth—but he was checked on three sides. As he scrambled to move his wagons and cattle south, toward Military Road, Price left Major General John S. Marmaduke to defend the Confederates' right flank, along the Big Blue River. He left Brigadier General Joseph O. Shelby to lead the attack on Curtis's forces along Brush Creek. General Curtis watched the battle unfold from the roof of the Harris House in Westport (which survives today as the Harris-Kearney House Museum).

The union forces advanced and were repelled twice; they were forming for a third try when a local farmer showed them a path to flank the Confederate left, near the Bent-Ward Home. The plateau and fields south of Brush Creek became killing fields as Pleasanton clawed his way across the Big Blue River, the thirty Union cannons tore up the center of the Confederate lines and Curtis turned the Confederate left. The Confederates were outnumbered,

Pleasanton's advance through Independence, Missouri, October 22, 1864. *Courtesy of the Westport Historical Society, photograph by Jay Rothman.*

John Wornall House Museum, 6115 Wornall Road, Kansas City, Missouri. *Courtesy of David W. Jackson, orderlypackrat.com.*

outgunned and out of options. Shelby fought and regrouped; then he fought some more to give the rest of Price's troops time to retreat, but the battle and the campaign were lost. The Confederates had been using the home of John Wornall as a hospital (also surviving as a museum today), but the Union troops took it over as they drove the Confederates out of town; they immediately used it for the same purpose.

The aftermath was horrific. Nearly three thousand (more than the population of either Westport or Kansas City at the time) wounded and dead men and horses were spread over miles of fields and forests. Many of the men didn't have uniforms, and many of the Confederates who did have uniforms were wearing the Union blues that they had taken at Glasgow and other battles. The Union troops pursued Price down the border, fighting the largest cavalry battle of the war at Mine Creek (where General Marmaduke and many of his men were captured), and, eventually, back into Southwest Missouri.

The war on the western border ended as it began: not with two gentlemen sitting down to sign some papers, but in a desperate, bloody, hopeless fight that only ended when one side couldn't go on.

CONSTITUTION HALL STATE HISTORIC SITE

319 Elmore Street
Lecompton, Kansas 66050
785-887-6520
www.kshs.org/p/constitution-hall-plan-your-visit/15523

TERRITORIAL CAPITOL MUSEUM

640 East Woodson Avenue
Lecompton, Kansas 66050
785-887-6148
www.lecomptonkansas.com

In the autumn of 1857, the Lecompton Constitutional Convention met and drafted a proslavery constitution in the upper story of this building. At the time, the first floor was being used as the U.S. Land Office, where thousands of settlers and speculators filed claims for the newly available land in the territory (after the Native Americans were either forced out or led off). The legislators that passed the Lecompton constitution were replaced, just a few weeks later, by an antislavery majority, who met in the same hall and began dismantling the laws that had been passed by their predecessors. The state's legislature moved to Lawrence in 1858, but the building in Lecompton continued to serve as the U.S. District Land Office until 1860. Since then, it has been used as a dry goods store, a hotel, a meeting hall, a college dormitory, a telephone office and even an undertaker's parlor. Since the building was purchased and donated to the state in 1986, it has been a State of Kansas Historic Site. The Territorial Capital Museum is housed in the former Lane University (named after notorious Senator James Lane) building. In 1854, Congress appropriated $50,000 to build this structure as the Kansas Territorial Capitol. However, the Border and Civil Wars halted work on the building, and Topeka became the state's capital in the interim. The building was finished in the 1860s, and it became Lane University. After operating as a college (where Dwight D. Eisenhower's parents went to school and met) for over thirty years, the building went through a series of uses and eventually became the Lane Museum. Today, the building is home to the Territorial Capital Museum; the museum chronicles the town's history, with cannonballs from the Bleeding Kansas period to artifacts from the present.

JOHN BROWN MUSEUM STATE HISTORIC SITE

Tenth and Main Streets (in John Brown Memorial Park)
Osawatomie, Kansas 66064
913-755-4384
www.osawatomieks.org

The Reverend Samuel Adair and his wife, Florella, lived in the abolitionist community of Osawatomie, Kansas, in a two-room cabin that is now a museum and Kansas State Historic Site in John Brown Park. The cabin was used by the Adairs as a stop on the Underground Railroad, and John Brown, who was Florella Adair's half brother, used the home as his headquarters during the Bleeding Kansas period. The Adair Home was moved to the John Brown Memorial Park (the site of the 1856 Battle of Osawatomie)

Samuel Adair Cabin, John Brown Memorial Park (moved from original site), Osawatomie, Miami County, Kansas. *Courtesy of the Library of Congress Prints and Photographs Division (HABS KANS,61-OSA,1—4).*

in 1912, and today, it features exhibits in both rooms, along with displays outside of the cabin. The cabin features furnishings and belongings of the Adair family, Civil War weapons and exhibits that interpret Brown's role in the Battle of Osawatomie.

QUINDARO UNDERGROUND RAILROAD MUSEUM

3436 North Twenty-Seventh Street
Kansas City, Kansas 66104
913-321-1220
www.visitkansascityks.com

This collection of artifacts and documents related to the town of Quindaro is housed in the Vernon Multipurpose Center. The first stop for slaves who were trying to escape Missouri was across the Missouri River, at the free port of Quindaro in the Kansas Territory. The town of Quindaro became a beacon of hope for African Americans who were searching for freedom and support from the Underground Railroad.

1859 JAIL, MARSHAL'S HOME AND MUSEUM

217 North Main Street
Independence, Missouri 64050
816-252-1892
www.jchs.org/1859-jail

"One of a kind" may be an overused phrase, but in this case, it is appropriate. The 1859 Jail, Marshal's Home and Museum was built during the Border War era; at one time, it housed William Quantrill, Frank James and other prisoners of war and civilians under Order No. 11. The jail also housed local miscreants who had spit on the sidewalk or committed similar petty crimes. Two Civil War battles pushed through the jail's doors, and hangings and shootouts took place on its grounds. The contrast of the period is palpable through the appointed Marshal's Home and the stone prison cells with iron doors. A young Tom Pendergast served as the deputy and marshal at the jail before his career as political boss in Kansas City landed him on the other side of the bars. Since the jail, which was used until 1933, is located in the

Jail and marshal's home, circa 1859, 217 North Main Street, Independence, Missouri. *Courtesy of David W. Jackson, orderlypackrat.com.*

historic Independence Square, visitors to Kansas City can easily step inside the cells, tour the marshal's office and living quarters and view displays of prisoner's homemade weapons, handcuffs and other objects. When the building was about to be demolished in the late 1950s, Harry S. Truman made the first call in the fundraising effort to save the jail as a museum. The Jackson County Historical Society maintains the museum and collection, and volunteers serve as staff members and docents. Every year, thousands of schoolchildren and tourists benefit from their efforts.

WATKINS MUSEUM OF HISTORY

1047 Massachusetts Street
Lawrence, Kansas 66044
785-841-4109
info@watkinsmuseum.org

The Watkins Museum houses thousands of artifacts; many of them are surviving pieces from the Border War era, including the Eldridge Chair, the Old Sacramento Cannon, Civil War swords and a John Brown pike.

BAKER UNIVERSITY AND OLD CASTLE MUSEUM

513 Fifth Street
Baldwin City, Kansas 66006
785-594-8380
www.bakeru.edu

This three-story limestone structure was built in 1858; known originally as the "College Building," today's Old Castle Museum was Kansas's first four-year university building. The Old Castle Museum currently contains artifacts and memorabilia from Methodist circuit riders, the Santa Fe Trail, early settlements and Baker University. This site also includes the Old Palmyra Post Office, which once served travelers along the Santa Fe Trail.

PONY EXPRESS MUSEUM

914 Penn Street
Saint Joseph, Missouri 64503
816-279-5059
www.ponyexpress.org

The Pony Express Museum in St. Joseph, Missouri, is a neat museum in a historic town. The museum's displays help tell the story of a short-lived, but ambitious, project to keep mail flowing before the invention of the telegraph.

LONE JACK BATTLEFIELD MUSEUM AND SOLDIER'S CEMETERY

301 South Bynum Road
Lone Jack, Missouri 64070
816-697-8833
www.historiclonejack.org/museum

Following the Confederate victory at the First Battle of Independence in early August 1862, Union troops mobilized, with the intention of combining the forces of three different posts to push the Rebels out of the border area. But the Union troops failed to converge before the rebels attacked a Union force of eight hundred men under the command of Major Emory Foster at the town of Lone Jack. Foster's men mistakenly believed that Quantrill, who was leading the Rebels, would take no prisoners. According to veterans of the battle, the ensuing fight was one of the most intense of the entire war—it was fought out of fear and desperation. Foster left the field with heavy losses, returning to Lexington, Missouri, with only half as many men as he set out with. Many of the dead from both sides were buried at the battle site. Today, the battle site is home to a cemetery and a stone museum, which displays of a variety of items related to local history, including artifacts from the battle, photos of the men who fought there and dioramas depicting scenes from the Civil War along the border.

BATTLE OF LEXINGTON STATE HISTORIC SITE

1101 Delaware Street
Lexington, Missouri 64067

This is the site of an early Confederate victory in the Civil War. The battle is sometimes called the Battle of the Hemp Bales, because the Confederate attackers rolled hemp bales in front of themselves, using them as cover as they moved toward the federal position.

LITTLE BLUE BATTLEFIELD

21594 East Old Lexington Road
Independence, Missouri

Although there is currently no museum at the site, the Battle of the Little Blue River Park is owned and operated by Jackson County Parks and Recreation. The site has two historic markers pertaining to the battle, a shelter house and access to the Little Blue Trace Trail. There is an additional marker in the park that describes General Blunt's position and the part of the battle that took place on the west of the park. The marker can be found on the north side of Highway 24, as you turn north on Blue Mills Road, then immediately west on the access road (sounds confusing, but it's visible from the highway, to the west of a big church and cemetery).

BIG BLUE BATTLEFIELD PARK

East Sixty-Third Street and Manchester Trafficway
Kansas City, Missouri 64130
816-513-7500
www.kcparks.org/places/big-blue-battlefield-park
www.battleofwestport.org/tours

The Big Blue Battlefield was a key part of the Battle of Westport. The fight took place on October 22, 1864, when Price's army was attempting to cross the Blue River. The next day, Pleasanton attacked the Confederates ensconced on the west bank, in the position they'd taken from the Kansas troops the day before. These positions made up the Big Blue and Byram's Ford Battlefields (a walking tour of Byram's Ford Battlefield is available through www.thecivilwarmuse.com). During the first engagement, the Confederates fought their way across the Blue River in order to secure an escape route for their wagons and cattle to the south of Kansas City. The next day, the Confederate army turned north, hoping to break through to Westport or, at least, push the federals back, but this all hinged on stopping Pleasanton from crossing the Blue River and flanking their forces. It was a tough fight, and there were several hundred casualties, but the federal forces ultimately prevailed and drove the last of the Confederate army out of Missouri.

JACOB L. LOOSE PARK

5200 Wornall Road
Kansas City, Missouri
www.kcparks.org/places/battle-of-westportmonument-2

Some of the most intense portions of the Battle of Westport took place in the area around Jacob L. Loose Park. There are several markers showing the various units' positions throughout the park, and, along with automobile and walking tours, you can find five geocache locations and waymarks in the park online. The Battle of Westport Monument, located north of the rose garden, commemorates the location where Major General Sterling Price, the "Old Fox" of the Confederate army, was defeated and his forces retreated to the Arkansas Territory. The six-ton red granite marker was dedicated in October 1953. Cannons are located nearby.

HARRIS-KEARNEY HOUSE MUSEUM

4000 Baltimore Avenue
Kansas City, Missouri 64111
816-561-1821
www.westporthistorical.com/harris-kearney-house

Built in 1855, the Harris-Kearney House is the headquarters of the Westport Historical Society. The home, dubbed the "Mansion," was originally built on the southwest corner of the intersection of Main Street and Westport Road, where it overlooked the busy Santa Fe Trail. After Harris died in 1873, his daughter, Josephine (Harris) Kearney, and son-in-law, Colonel Charles E. Kearney, moved their family into the home and built an addition to accommodate their five children. The house stayed in the Kearney family into the next century. In 1922, the house was saved and moved one block, to its current location. The Westport Historical Society hosts exhibits and events in the home throughout the year, and they operate a library, archives and publications on the history of Westport.

THE JOHN WORNALL HOUSE

6115 Wornall Road
Kansas City, Missouri 64113
816-444-1858
www.wornallmajors.org

The Wornall Home, built in 1858, was owned by a successful farmer named John Wornall, who sold his crops in nearby Westport. He was a Southerner and had five slaves at the start of the Civil War, but he declared neutrality and, at one point during the war, even began paying his slaves. However, Wornall's slaves eventually left his estate, most likely heading to freedom in Kansas. The home, at separate points, served as a hospital for both sides during the Battle of Westport. Today, the Wornhall Home is one of the few antebellum structures left in the area; it is furnished with many period pieces and several of the Wornalls' personal belongings. The Wornall Home is a real gem, with beautifully maintained gardens, and it should be on any history lover's short list when visiting the area.

BINGHAM-WAGGONER ESTATE

313 West Pacific Avenue
Independence, Missouri 64050
816-461-3491
www.bwestate.net

In the 1830s, a small gristmill was built in Independence, near one of the public freshwater springs. Across the road, John Lewis built a fine home on a hill, with a view of Independence Square. His land was traversed by thousands heading out on the Santa Fe Trail and, later, the Oregon and California Trails. In fact, impressive wagon ruts were left in the field of the nineteen-acre estate, and they remain to this day. George Caleb Bingham, Missouri's most notable nineteenth-century artist and politician, was the home's most famous resident. The Bingham-Waggoner Estate's residents watched the Second Battle of Independence from the balcony of the

Lewis-Bingham-Waggoner Estate, 313 West Pacific Avenue, Independence, Missouri. *Courtesy of Paul Kirkman.*

home. In 1867, Peter Waggoner and his family purchased the "old City mill" from John Overfelt. The Waggoners began milling flour in the mill and developed a reputation for quality, producing "Queen of the Pantry" flour. With success came expansion and an 1890s remodel of the home. The Waggoner family lived on the estate until 1976. Today, the Bingham-Waggoner Historical Society, in cooperation with the City of Independence, owns and operates the estate, which exhibits 90 percent of the Waggoner family's original furnishings, carpets and paintings. Across the street is the National Frontier Trails Museum, and several other sites are located in the nearby Independence Square.

Read More

Action Before Westport, 1864, by Howard N. Monnett
The Battle of Westport: Missouri's Great Confederate Raid, by Paul Kirkman
Blood on the Streets: The Civil War Comes to Jackson County, Missouri, August 1862, by Ralph A. Monaco II
John Brown, Abolitionist, by David S. Reynolds
LOCK DOWN: Outlaws, Lawmen and Frontier Justice in Jackson County, Missouri, by David Jackson and Paul Kirkman
Midnight Rising, by Tony Horwitz
The Pony Express: The History and Legacy of America's Most Famous Mail Service, by Charles River
Riders of the Pony Express, by Ralph Moody
Westport, Missouri's Port of Many Returns, by Patricia Cleary Miller

5

BACK TO BUSINESS

The Civil War had taken an enormous toll on the communities near the Missouri River's bend. The number of lives lost, families and homes destroyed and fortunes reversed during that time has (thankfully) been unequaled. Everything had changed, and the cadre of leading families in Kansas City had been divided and diminished in the process.

It is to the city's credit that a group of forward-thinking individuals rose from the ashes and cleared the way forward. Foremost among these individuals was the trio of Charles E. Kearney, Robert T. Van Horn and Kersey Coates; these men drove the effort to connect Kansas City to Chicago with a bridge over the Missouri River. Had they dawdled or delayed, it is likely that either Leavenworth, Atchison or St. Joseph would have been first to bridge the Missouri, and Kansas City may have floundered as the West's trails were replaced by rails.

The men persuaded the railroad to build a cutoff at Cameron to Kansas City, Missouri, selling the idea that it could save the later expense of having to build a second bridge over the Kaw River. Leavenworth was close to making a deal at the time, but the group from Kansas City offered the railroad a good price on land in the West Bottoms that they had been buying up in anticipation of securing an agreement. The Kansas City bridge, or Hannibal Bridge (named, in part, after the controlling railroad), was constructed under the stewardship of engineer Octave Chanute. It completed the link between the Chicago markets and Texas cattle ranches when it opened on July 3, 1869, and it helped establish Kansas City as the dominant city of the region.

Union-Confederate Monument site, 227 East Twenty-Eighth Street Terrace, Kansas City, Missouri. *Courtesy of the Library of Congress Prints and Photographs Division (HALS MO-1-A-1).*

The project began in 1867 and was completed in 1869, to enormous fanfare, as forty thousand spectators, governors and dignitaries joined the celebration. The event started with a parade led by a brass band, which was followed by a balloon ascension and speakers. In the classic Kansas City style, the celebration concluded with a massive barbecue that was laid out for everyone in attendance. The feast was, no doubt, washed down with appropriate libations.

In the same year, the exuberant city became the home of a baseball team called the Kansas City Antelopes. The team had played its local rivals, the Atchison Pomeroys, once, at Atchison; the game ended early in a brawl, with Atchison fans thoroughly beating the umpire and bloodying the Antelopes. Another game between the teams was set to be played in Kansas City, but finding an umpire who would face the violent crowds proved to be difficult. Fortunately, deputy U.S. marshal James Butler Hickok was a fan of the game and volunteered for the job. The usually rowdy crowd showed up for the game, but as Wild Bill Hickok called the game, they seemed exceptionally well behaved and quiet. This may have been because Hickok's reputation preceded him, but it also could have been the pair of loaded colt revolvers the umpire wore throughout the game that convinced both the players and fans not to argue his calls. The Antelopes won the game, and Hickok rode off the field in a carriage that was on its way to the saloons to celebrate.

The end of the Civil War and the arrival of the railroad brought the potential of prosperity to the area. The farms and communities' produce could now be transported to eager markets in the East. The influx of Texas cattle, new stockyards (also designed by Chanute), the cattle exchange and the meat processing facilities firmly secured Kansas City's economic future well into the twentieth century. The Kansas City Stockyards, located in the area known as the West Bottoms, grew from 1871 to be the second-largest stockyards in the country. At their height, the Kansas City Stockyards

Kansas City stockyards, circa 1906, Kansas City, Missouri. *Courtesy of the Library of Congress Prints and Photographs Division (LC-DIG-det-4a13246).*

processed over two million cattle a year. Dozens of railroad lines fanned out from the city, hauling cattle and grain to markets throughout the country and bringing ever more settlers to the wide-open West.

In 1878, the Union Depot was built between Union Street and the West Bottoms; at the time, eight different railroad lines serviced the area. The depot was conveniently located for hauling cattle, but it was less than ideal for passengers. The area around the station was covered in soot from all the coal-powered steam engines of the surrounding factories; the area was also surrounded by the bawdy houses, tattoo parlors and saloons that had sprung up to serve the rowdy cowboys and hardworking, hard-drinking laborers in the slaughterhouses and meatpacking plants.

The roads up from the Missouri River were dug out of breaks in the cliffs, so Kansas City was nicknamed Gully Town. Housing near the stockyards, and the meatpacking plants that grew up with them, were built quickly and cheaply to accommodate the thousands of immigrants who came to live and work in the booming area. A shanty town was built on muddy paths, up through cliffs; it was covered in soot, reeked of cattle and were bustling with nefarious characters. This was the first impression that passengers had of Kansas City when they left the train station. The ascension to the newer portions of town involved a stomach-churning ride on the cable cars up the steep Ninth-Street incline. The wealthy were above it all, settling into new homes in the area that lowlanders derisively called Silk Stocking Hill, but developer Kersey Coates dubbed the area Quality Hill. (This community was set atop a two-hundred-foot bluff on the west side of downtown. It was bounded by Broadway Boulevard to the east, Interstate 35 to the west, Seventh Street to the north and Fourteenth Street to the south).

The population of the town had grown from four thousand in 1860 to thirty thousand by the 1870s. The Gully Town population consisted mostly of freed slaves who had come northward and poor immigrants who were primarily from Italy, Germany and Ireland. Each of these groups had members that pushed out into new neighborhoods, escaping the bottoms and building distinct communities that worked toward advancing and taking care of their own people. Neighborhoods like Columbus Park (Italian American), Eighteenth and Vine (African American), Strawberry Hill (Croatian American) and Argentine (Mexican-American) all grew out of the push to move out of the bottoms and build working- and middle-class communities in the late nineteenth century. The Irish were the largest group of immigrants in Kansas City in the 1870s, and their influence at the ballot was capitalized on by politicians for decades; however, the immigrant experience in Kansas City was familiar to many of its post–Civil War inhabitants.

The rapid growth of the city, spawned by the railroads and meatpacking industry, led to many of its citizens obtaining fortunes. While this new class of wealthy community leaders built its mansions, many in the working class dug in and scratched their way out of poverty to build the city and its middle class. Not everyone was blessed by or ready to embrace Kansas City's new economy. Young men from families who had been wealthy and successful in the old slave economy found themselves shut out of polite society at every level. The guerrilla bands had lost their leaders, but many of the members had no intention of cowing to the railroads, Union men and bankers who seemed to own so many of the farms and homes that had belonged to their friends and family members before the Civil War. The ex-guerrillas and former Confederates found their voices in the fiery rhetoric of the *Kansas City Times*; the paper was edited by John Newman Edwards, who had been an adjutant for Confederate general Jo Shelby during the Civil War.

On February 13, 1866, the first daylight bank robbery took place at the Clay County Savings and Loan in Liberty, Missouri (a few miles north of Kansas City). Among those accused of the crime were Frank and Jesse James of Kearney, Missouri. The gang left with nearly $60,000 in cash and certificates (a haul worth nearly $1 million today), but as the group of men rode away from the scene, they fired off several rounds to create a diversion. During the escape, the men shot and killed a seventeen-year-old college student named George Wymore, who, ironically, was a student at William Jewell College, a university that the James brothers' father, Robert James, had helped found. The gang hurried to the Missouri River, where they boarded a ferry boat and crossed the river before a posse could catch up with them. The bank could never recoup its losses and eventually closed.

For nearly twenty years, hundreds of lawmen, posses, private investigators and bounty hunters tried to capture the James Gang, but time and time again, the brothers eluded them, often with the help of like-minded ex-rebels and wisely silent country folk. Jesse fed into his own myth and used it to his advantage; Edwards, a *Kansas City Times* editor, would pass on stories—real or imagined—about the gang's generosity with their ill-gotten gains. Jesse James had taken part in violent guerrilla warfare from his early teen years until the end of the Civil War. It's claimed that he was shot by Union soldiers while trying to surrender immediately after the war; it was confirmed that

Above: The Jesse James Home, 21216 Jesse James Farm Road, Kearney, Clay County, Missouri. *Courtesy of David W. Jackson, orderlypackrat.com.*

Left: Jesse James's grave, Kearney, Clay County, Missouri. *Courtesy of David W. Jackson, orderlypackrat.com.*

he was shot in the chest around that time. James likely robbed his first bank before he was twenty years old; he and his brother Frank were accused of robbing trains, stagecoaches and banks in multiple states (sometimes in two places at once) from 1865 until Jesse was murdered by a gang member in St. Joseph in 1882.

Missouri governor and former Union colonel Thomas Crittenden approved a railroad bounty of $10,000 each for Jesse and Frank James, private citizens who had not been tried or convicted of any crime. Gang member Robert Ford and his brother, Charlie, agreed to try to assassinate Jesse James, with the promise of reward money and a pardon for past crimes. Jesse was living under an assumed name in St. Joseph, when the brothers, who had gained his trust to some degree, saw their opportunity to assassinate him. Bob Ford shot James in the back while he was reaching to adjust a picture frame. The Fords wired Governor Crittenden asking for the reward and turned themselves in. Instead of a reward, they were charged with first-degree murder and were tried and sentenced to death by hanging on the same day. Crittenden responded with a pardon two hours after the trial. Widely criticized for the move, the Northern Democrat and former Union colonel was replaced in the next election by Southern Democrat and former Confederate general John S. Marmaduke (who ran as a proud ex-Confederate who supported railroad regulation). In Kansas City, Missouri, the old Democratic Party, with many ex-rebels in its ranks, used the Jesse James incident to regain dominance; they even later embraced Jesse James's son and helped him through law school. (James's grandson became a lawyer and judge in California).

The pie in Kansas City was getting bigger, and everyone was vying for a piece.

PATEE HOUSE MUSEUM

1202 Penn Street
St. Joseph, Missouri 64503
816-232-8206
patee@ponyexpress.net

The Patee House was a luxury hotel built in 1858; at the time, it also housed the offices of the Pony Express. It went through a number of reincarnations and owners, but it eventually served the longest as a garment factory. Today, the Patee House's grounds are a smorgasbord for history lovers, with two museums, multiple displays and an old-fashioned carousel and saloon. Readers shouldn't miss a chance to run up to St. Joseph.

JESSE JAMES HOME MUSEUM

1201 South Twelfth Street
St. Joseph, Missouri 64503
816-232-8206
www.stjoemo.info/362/Jesse-James-Home

Owned and operated by the Pony Express Historical Association, the Jesse James Home is the house where Jesse James was assassinated by Robert Ford in 1882. It was moved in 1939 from its original location (1318 Lafayette Street, St. Joseph, Missouri), and it was moved again in 1977, to a resting place directly behind the Patee House Museum, where it remains today. The Jesse James Home's exhibits focus on the life and death of Jesse James. When Jesse James's body was exhumed in 1995 for DNA testing, several artifacts were recovered from the grave and are now on display. Among these artifacts are the coffin handles, a small tie pin that Jesse James was wearing the day he was killed, a bullet removed from James's right lung area and a casting of his skull that shows a bullet hole behind his right ear.

JESSE JAMES BIRTHPLACE

21216 James Farm Road
Kearney, Missouri 64060
816-736-8500
www.jessejamesmuseum.org
www.jessejames.org

The farm where Frank and Jesse James grew up, and where their mother and other family members continued to live for generations, was sold by the James family to Clay County in 1978 for the purpose of making it a historic site that is available to the public. The Friends of the James Farm was organized shortly after the farm was opened to visitors; it assists the county in its efforts to restore and preserve the farm and home. Guided tours of the farmhouse are offered at the site and start with an introductory film about the James family. Today, the home features displays of the James family's furnishings and personal effects, and the museum includes exhibits of guns and the boots that Jesse was wearing when he was killed by Bob Ford. His original tombstone is on the farm; it reads, "Jesse W. James, Died April 3, 1882, Aged 34 years, 6 months, 28 days, Murdered by a traitor and a coward whose name is not worthy to appear here." He was later moved to the family plot at Mount Olivet Cemetery in Kearney, Missouri. (Although there has been a continuing controversy that asserts Jesse faked his death and moved to Texas, where he died at the age of 103, but the author of this book is not pulling that thread.) The farm's gift shop sells several books about the brothers and their times as outlaws. The Jesse James Birthplace Museum has two small research libraries that are available by appointment only.

JESSE JAMES BANK MUSEUM

103 North Water Street
Liberty, Missouri 64068
816-736-8510
www.claycountymo.gov/Historic_Sites/Jesse_James_Bank_Museum

Located on the historic square in Liberty, Missouri, the Jesse James Bank Museum was the site of the first successful peacetime bank robbery that took place in daylight. While the robbers were never caught, the crime was believed to have been pulled off by the James Gang. The bank has been restored to reflect how it looked in 1866, when the gang robbed it and left with guns blazing.

CONFEDERATE MEMORIAL STATE PARK (FORMERLY THE CONFEDERATE SOLDIERS HOME OF MISSOURI)

211 West First Street
Higginsville, Missouri 64037-8158
660-584-2853
www.mostateparks.com/park/confederate-memorial-state-historic-site

The beautiful grounds of the Confederate Memorial State Historic Site were once the location of the Confederate Soldiers Home of Missouri, which provided housing for 1,600 Civil War veterans and their families over the course of sixty years. The site is comprised of a restored chapel, a cemetery and three other historic buildings. Established by Missourians who were concerned for the welfare of aging and ill Confederate veterans, the home accepted any veteran who had served in the Confederate army, including members of guerrilla groups. The land for the home was donated by a pro-Union farmer, and Union veterans' groups helped raise funds to provide housing for their former enemies. The men grew some of their own food on the land, and they built a sort of community for themselves. The last Confederate soldier living there passed away in 1950, at the age of 108. Today, in addition to the buildings and cemetery, the site's more than one hundred acres contain numerous lakes to fish in, as well as walking trails and places to picnic.

LIVESTOCK EXCHANGE AND KANSAS CITY STOCKYARDS

1600 Genessee Street
Kansas City, Missouri 64102
816-221-4501
www.livestockexchangebldg.com

The Kansas City Stockyards drove Kansas City's economy for over one hundred years, but the changing methods of shipment, environmental concerns and devastating floods contributed to the stockyards' decline and final closure in the 1990s. But with the loss of the stockyards came some gains; the new owners found a cache of historic documents boxed up in the old stock exchange building that were contributed to the Kansas City Public Library, and they are now held and curated by the library's Missouri Valley Special Collections. Today, the building and surrounding area have experienced an economic revitalization, as trendy restaurants have popped up alongside reworked originals, like the longtime exchange building restaurant, the Golden Ox. For those who want to experience the old stockyards area (minus the smell), check out the Livestock Exchange Building. When it was built in 1911, the Livestock Exchange Building was the largest livestock exchange building in the world. There are several restaurants and new apartment communities in the area, along with the Stockyard Brewery, for visitors to mosey around and enjoy.

Read More

The Bandit Rides Again, by Ralph A. Monaco II
Civil War on the Missouri-Kansas Border, by Donald L. Gilmore
Cowtown: Cattle Trails and West Bottom Tales, by Edward T. Matheny Jr.
Frank and Jesse James, by Ted P. Yeatman
Jesse James and the Civil War in Missouri, by Robert L. Dyer
Jesse James and the Lost Cause, by James P. Muehlberger
Jesse James: Last Rebel of the Civil War, by T.J. Stiles
Son of a Bandit: Jesse James and the Leeds Gang, by Ralph A. Monaco II
Twenty Years of Kansas City's Live Stock Trade, by Powell Cuthbert
West Side Kansas City, by William J. Craig

6

LOOKING FORWARD

The rapid growth of Kansas City as a railroad hub and shipping center sparked expansion along the Missouri River. Communities grew up the bluffs and into the surrounding fields and forestland, from which some of the city's earliest streets were named: Walnut, Oak, Cherry and Locust. Speculators bought and sold land in anticipation of the growth, and many of the area's early arrivals, who had originally purchased land for next to nothing, were, all of a sudden, worth a fortune. The Coates Addition, named after its developer, Kersey Coates, was the first of many planned expansions in Kansas City. The Kansas City Stockyards were a starting point of trade, but the railroads hauled all sorts of commodities through Kansas City's central hub, and the city became a center for the storage and distribution of wholesale commodities and grain.

The expansion of the city in every direction followed the growth of the railroads, and hopeful developers sought to lure investment dollars and new communities to the surrounding countryside. Colonel Harvey Merrick Vaile and his wife, Sophia, moved to Kansas City, Missouri, in 1859. Vaile was a staunch abolitionist who had helped found the Republican Party in Kansas City. He had already had success investing in the construction of the Erie Canal, and he was a part-owner of the Star Mail Routes, with rights to the route to Santa Fe. Vaile was one of many local investors who experienced success upon success. In 1871, construction started on his thirty-two-room mansion in Independence; the home cost $150,000 ($4 million in 2019). Vaile was not alone in his success; families who had lived in log cabins or

Vaile Victorian mansion, Independence, Missouri. *Courtesy of the Library of Congress Prints and Photographs Division (LC-DIG-highsm-13272).*

shacks just a few decades before were building empires and mansions in the late nineteenth century.

The Kansas City Stockyards connected the United States' eastern and southwestern markets like never before; this was largely due to the expansion of the railroads. The late nineteenth century was also the age of the lumber barons; Kansas City's Long family was one of several successful lumber families in the area. Kansas City's growing importance as a railroad hub, connecting western resources with eastern markets, was complemented by an expansion of its industry. Local manufacturers often recruited foreign laborers to come to the Kansas City area when the local workforce wasn't sufficient. Waves of immigration throughout the late nineteenth and early twentieth centuries continued to grow the community and contribute to its strength and diversity.

At first, some of the local breweries built rail lines to move their products and workers; they later built amusement parks and other attractions to draw customers away from the city center on the trolley lines or short rail lines they'd built. The Heim Brewery built two electric parks in Kansas City. The first was built near the Heim Brewery in the East Bottoms in 1896; it had a beer garden with beer piped straight in from the brewery next door. The second and much larger electric park was built at Forty-Sixth and Paseo Streets. It had a train that circled around the grounds, and fireworks were set off at the end of the night—sound familiar? A regular customer of the park was young Walt Disney, who lived a mile or so away, at 3028 Bellefontaine Street. The park had concessions, musical shows, arcades, rides and landscaping to accentuate it all. Disney must have paid close attention, as just thirty years later, he built Disneyland and incorporated all of these features.

In 1880, William Rockhill Nelson moved to Kansas City and began publishing the *Kansas City Star*, an advance subscription newspaper that, under his guidance, grew to dominate the local market. Nelson's *Star* became a crusading voice in the Kansas City area, attacking local corruption and actively advocating for civic improvements including a municipal auditorium and park system. He was one of many voices promoting civic improvements. The City Beautiful Movement, which had been started in the 1890s, had

Walt Disney with Mickey Mouse drawing. *Courtesy of the Library of Congress Prints and Photographs Division (LC-DIG-hec-36581).*

behind it a concern for the health and well-being of the country's growing urban communities. Urban planning was, in many ways, still in its infancy, but civic leaders in Kansas City embraced the ideology and began funding an ambitious park and boulevards system that would link various parts of the city with green spaces.

In 1876, James Pendergast opened his saloon in the West Bottoms; it was named Climax after the racehorse that had won Pendergast the money he used to build his business. His younger brother, Tom, came to work at the saloon in 1894. James had been elected alderman of Kansas City's first ward, and for the next forty years, the Pendergast family expanded their political power in the city, the state of Missouri and beyond. It was not unusual for saloon owners to be well known and popular in the communities they served. In poorer communities, the saloon may have been the only place to cash a check or get a loan, as banks generally followed the wealthy to the suburbs.

The Pendergasts' machine provided holiday meals, Election Day buffets and financial services (check cashing and loans) to Kansas city's working-class communities in order to garner as much goodwill and votes as it could from them. In addition to these services, the machine organized sporting and social clubs and events for the white-collar workers who were often kept out of the exclusive Northeast and Country Club communities. Where attempts to gain goodwill failed, the machine was more than willing to use violence and intimidation to retain or expand its power. In 1896, Tom Pendergast was appointed deputy marshal under former Confederate Sam Chiles, and in 1902, he succeeded Chiles as Jackson County's marshal. His big brother James was using his influence to get his family members and friends elected or appointed to city and county government positions. Tom learned the family business and ultimately took over as Jim's health declined.

In 1887, R.A. Long moved the Long-Bell Lumber Company's headquarters to Kansas City, and over the next several years, he expanded the business to employ workers from all over the country. Long's seventy-two-room mansion at 3218 Gladstone Boulevard was built in 1910; it is now the Kansas City Museum. Long's farm is located south of town, in Lee's Summit; it was once a magnificent showplace. The 2,000-acre farm had forty-two buildings, 250 acres of landscaped gardens and four greenhouses. Today, Longview Lake and Longview College are located on portions of the original farm. Long owned a number of lumber yards, pieces of land and sawmills from Louisiana to Washington State. Like many of Kansas City's successful entrepreneurs, Long gave back to society; he even led fundraising efforts to build the Liberty Memorial.

Corinthian Hall, Kansas City Museum of History and Science. *Courtesy of the Library of Congress Prints and Photographs Division (HABS MO,48-KANCI,9—15 (CT)).*

Long built his home at the north end of the City in an area developed by the Scarritt family, whose members were descendants of early Westport settler Reverend Nathan Scarritt (whose home at 4038 Central Street still stands). After Reverend Scarritt passed away, the Kansas City Parks Department acquired some of his land in the northeast community of Cliff Drive, which is now a state scenic byway. Many of the parks and institutions in the city were built on land developed or contributed by the leading families of Kansas City. Kansas City's tradition of philanthropy is rooted in the success and character of its late nineteenth- and early twentieth-century first families. One of the numerous examples of this philanthropy is that of Colonel Thomas Swope's donation of 1,334 acres to the city's park system in 1896.

The late nineteenth- and early twentieth-century movers and shakers in Kansas City consolidated power through political, financial and social networks on a level that is hard to imagine today. Men like Long, Pendergast and even J.C. Hall, the founder of Hallmark cards, rose rapidly from the bottom to the top of Kansas City's power structure, and they had friends and connections in every level of society. Pendergast held court in his offices

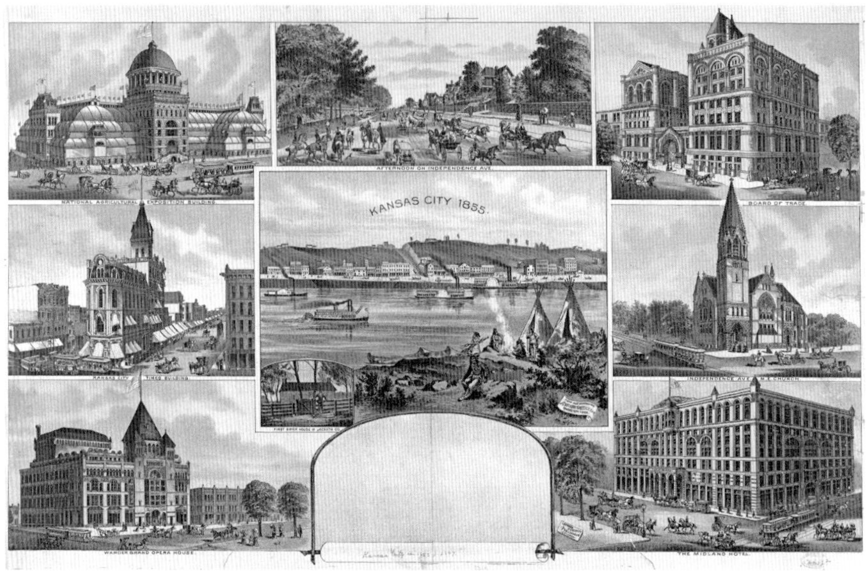

Kansas City, circa 1855 and 1887, Lanward Specialty Publishing Co., Chicago, Illinois. *Courtesy of the Library of Congress Prints and Photographs Division (LC 2005694440).*

at 1908 Main Street, and anyone, from the wealthiest magnate to the poorest immigrant, could present his or her requests directly to the seat of power on a first-come-first-served basis. The leadership of Kansas City was capable of cooperative effort, and with the assistance of newspaper publisher William Rockhill Nelson, made great strides in civic improvement.

Between 1880 and 1910, Kansas City's population tripled; the city added a new courthouse, library, federal building, city hall, parks system, city hospital, children's hospital, zoo and massive Union Station. Though the city's diverse community was made up of several large and distinct ethnic populations, the immigrant experience was shared by many of them. These groups merged in public but maintained their distinct heritages and formed strong communities around them.

VAILE VICTORIAN MANSION

1500 North Liberty Street
Independence, Missouri 64050
816-325-7430
www.vailemansion.org

This thirty-one-room mansion was built over the course of ten years (1871–81) for Colonel Harvey Vaille and his wife, Sophia. Harvey Vaille made his fortune investing in various businesses, including the construction of the Erie Canal and the Star Mail Routes, and he put much of that fortune into the bricks and mortar that were used to build his beloved wife, Sophia, the mansion of her dreams. Vaile was a prominent figure in Independence, Missouri's business and social circles, and his grand home hosted dignitaries from all over the country when they visited the area. After his heirs sold the home in 1908, it became a sanatorium that was subsequently converted into a nursing home. The home was later acquired by the City of Independence in 1983, and the mansion was restored to serve as a museum. Today, you can meander through the Vailles' home and enjoy its beautiful paintings, marble fireplaces and ornate decorations from another era.

INDEPENDENCE CHICAGO & ALTON DEPOT

318 West Pacific Avenue
Independence, Missouri 64050
www.chicagoaltondepot1879.org

Chicago & Alton Train Depot, Independence, Missouri. *Courtesy of Paul Kirkman.*

BLUE SPRINGS CHICAGO & ALTON (C&A) DEPOT

1108 Southwest Walnut
Blue Springs, Missouri 64050
www.bluespringshistory.org

If the trains of days gone by are your thing, local preservationists have saved a two-story 1879 C&A Depot in Independence, Missouri. They have also preserved an 1878 C&A Hotel and a one-story 1920s depot in Blue Springs. The Independence station is located on the grounds of the National Frontier Trails Museum. The Blue Springs Historical Society maintains the Chicago & Alton Depot and the two other sites in town.

UNION STATION KANSAS CITY

30 West Pershing Road
Kansas City, Missouri 64108
www.unionstation.org

If those C&A Depots didn't blow your stack, just wait until your train (or car) pulls into the 850,000-square-foot architectural masterpiece of Union Station in Kansas City. The station was built in 1914, saved from demolition in 1996 and reopened in 1999. While Union Station was once the hub of east–west rail activity for the nation, today, it "draws tourists from all over the world who marvel at her Grand Hall's 95-foot ceiling, three 3,500-pound chandeliers and 6-foot-wide clock hanging in her central arch." Today, the station is the home of Amtrak, restaurants, a planetarium, Science City, giant screen movies, a live theater and much more. All aboard!

SWOPE PARK AND SWOPE MEMORIAL

East Meyer Boulevard and Swope Parkway
Kansas City, Missouri 64132
www.kcparks.org/places/swope-park

Local capitalist-turned-philanthropist Colonel Thomas Hunton Swope donated 1,334 acres to the City of Kansas City in 1896. The land was so far from the city that visitors had to take a streetcar ride to get to there. (The city has a cool streetcar today, but you'll have to check its current routing—it doesn't go to Swope Park.) Today, Swope Park has grown to 1,805 acres and is the home of the Kansas City Zoo, Starlight Theatre, Lakeside Nature Center, golf courses, walking and equestrian trials, Lake of the Woods, the Southeast Community Center and the Swope Memorial, where the good colonel was laid to rest after his mysterious death in 1909. It is said that Swope Park is the second-largest urban park in the United States. Do you know the first? Is it Central Park in New York City? Guess again!

UNITY VILLAGE

400 Unity Circle North, Suite A
Lee's Summit, Missouri 64086
816-524-7414
www.unityworldwideministries.org

The world headquarters of the Unity Church, which describes itself as having no particular creed, no set dogma and no required ritual, and believes that there is good in every approach to God, has a beautiful campus and former farm in Lees Summit, Missouri. Anyone interested in the history of this organization, which dates back to the 1800s, can visit and check out its bookstore, classes and other services at Unity Village.

Unity School of Christianity, Unity Village, Missouri. *Courtesy of David W. Jackson, orderlypackrat.com.*

HALLMARK VISITORS CENTER AND CROWN CENTER

2501 McGee Trafficway
Kansas City, Missouri 64108
www.hallmark.com

J.C. Hall and his brothers started selling picture postcards out of shoeboxes at their local YMCA after they arrived in Kansas City from Nebraska in 1910. Seven years later, they had "invented" modern gift wrap, and the Hallmark brand was officially sealed in 1928. Hallmark was licensed by former Kansas Citian Walt Disney in 1932. Over the years, Hallmark has led the industry with signature marketing for "When You Care Enough to Send the Very Best." Kansas Citians have enjoyed Crown Center and Hall's luxury department stores, where Norman Rockwell's 1951 *Kansas City Spirit* oil painting is prominently exhibited. Hallmark Kaleidoscope invites children to be creative, have fun and feel good about their own ideas.

KANSAS CITY MUSEUM AND CORINTHIAN HALL

3218 Gladstone Boulevard
Kansas City, Missouri 64123
www.kansascitymuseum.org

LONGVIEW MANSION

1200 Southwest Longview Park Drive
Lee's Summit, Missouri 64081
www.longviewmansion.com

The former Beaux-Arts residence of the Robert A. Long family, Corinthian Hall, has been the home of the Kansas City Museum since 1940. Restored and open in 2020 for its twenty-first-century future, the museum captures the spirit of the Long family with an engaging set of exhibits that tell the his- and her-story of Kansas City. Separately discussed is the museum's curatorship of the Historic Garment District Museum downtown. And if visitors happen to jaunt out to the suburbs, they should check out the

Longs' "country home," the Longview Mansion. Today, it is an independent destination venue that was, in the mid-1900s, touted as the World's Most Beautiful Farm. Both of Longs' mansions have undergone multi million-dollar restorations.

STRAWBERRY HILL MUSEUM

720 North Fourth Street
Kansas City, Kansas 66101
www.strawberryhillmuseum.org

SUGAR CREEK HISTORICAL MUSEUM

606 North Sterling Avenue
Sugar Creek, Missouri 64054
816-254-3742

The Strawberry Hill Ethnic Cultural Society, founded in 1988, promotes, sponsors and preserves the heritage of the many nationalities and ethnicities that are prevalent throughout the many immigrant communities of Kansas City. The society has also saved and restored a fantastic Victorian Queen Anne–style home, where it showcases its exhibits and hosts events. The museum has a tearoom and a gift shop with numerous items from eastern Europe. Less grandiose, but equally as important, is the ethnic and cultural history preserved at the Sugar Creek Historical Museum in Sugar Creek, Missouri.

SPANISH-AMERICAN WAR MEMORIAL

South of Liberty Memorial Mall and Memorial Drive
Kansas City, Missouri
www.kcparks.org/places/the-hiker

The Hiker (1947) stands south of the Liberty Memorial Mall and represents veterans of the Spanish-American War, the Philippine Insurrection and the China Relief Expedition. The soldiers of these events were called hikers. Sculpted by Theo Alice Ruggles Kitson, the *Hiker* was one of several statues she created, and they are all placed throughout the United States. *The Hiker* is definitely looking forward! Are you?

THANK YOU, WALT DISNEY

1127 East Thirty-First Street
Kansas City, Missouri 64109
www.thankyouwaltdisney.org

The birthplace of Mickey Mouse is in jeopardy of being lost, but a local group called Thank You, Walt Disney Inc. is trying to save the building. The goal of the group is to maintain the first-class museum dedicated to Walt Disney's beginnings and how Hollywood animation was born in Kansas City. Today, you can drive by several Disney-related sites, including where "Walt Disney founded his first professional film studio at a building designed by noted Kansas City architect Nelle Peters in May 1922. He incorporated his new company with the Missouri secretary of state's office. He called it 'Laugh-O-gram Films.' The business operated on the second floor of the new [McConahay] Building at 1127 East Thirty-First Street, just a block east of Troost and a couple of blocks west of the Paseo. At one point, Walt employed eleven people and occupied five rooms on the west end of the second floor of the building." The group thanks you for your support and, as the famous mouse says, hopes to "see you real soon!"

KANSAS CITY, MISSOURI PARKS, RECREATION AND BOULEVARDS ARCHIVES

4600 East Sixty-Third Street Trafficway
Kansas City, MO 64130-4629
Kcparks.org/archives

The archive's collection includes architectural drawings, photographs, maps, microfilm and documents that catalogue the development of Kansas City's Parks and Boulevards system. Through the leadership of businessman August Meyer, the advocacy of *Kansas City Star* editor William

Rockhill Nelson and the direction of landscape architect George Kessler, Kansas City grew toward the goal of becoming a "city within a park." The history of Kansas City's many parks, which are connected by landscaped boulevards and greenways, is a legacy that is chronicled and made available through the archives.

Read More

The Chicago & Alton Railroad: The Only Way, by Gene Glendinning
A City Within a Park, by Jane Mobley and Nancy Whitnell Harris
Corinthian Hall: An American Palace, by Lenore K. Bradley
Deaths on Pleasant Street: The Ghastly Enigma of Colonel Swope and Doctor Hyde, by Giles Fowler
Hallmark: A Century of Caring, by Patrick Regan
Houses of Missouri, 1870–1940, by Cydney Millstein and Carol Grove
The Kansas City Spirit: Stories of Service Above Self, by Bruce Mathews
A Legacy of Design, by Janice Lee, David Boutros, Charlotte R. White and Deon Wolfenbarger
Longview Farm: Biography of a Dream Come True, by Teresa Thornton Mitchell
A Splendid Ride: The Streetcars of Kansas City, 1870–1957, by Monroe Dodd
Sugar Creek (Images of America), by Richard N. Piland
Union Station Kansas City, by Jeffrey Spivak
The Vaile Mansion: Hidden Secrets, by Cornell DeVille
Walt Disney's Missouri: The Roots of a Creative Genius, by Brian Burnes

7

TOM'S TOWN

Tom Pendergast never held a higher political office than alderman, but at the height of his power, his influence extended well beyond Kansas City. The Missouri governor's mansion had been dubbed Uncle Tom's Cabin, and he was courted by politicians on the national stage. While other parts of the country suffered through the Great Depression, Kansas City's economy stayed afloat, as William Rockhill Nelson and Pendergast advocated for civic improvements, and Pendergast provided the concrete, labor force and votes necessary to keep the projects going. To those who were allies of the machine—or at least stayed out of its way—Tom's Town was a well-run moneymaker, and the civic leaders of the city could count on Tom's support for improvement and infrastructure projects. Sure, the machine used intimidation and committed voting fraud and other crimes that have plagued society for centuries, but the dark side of machine politics had not truly emerged from the shadows. Prohibition, followed by the Great Depression, released it. The rise of criminal gangs, who warred over alcohol profits in the 1920s, and the desperate economic circumstances of the 1930s pushed many cities, including Tom's Town, to look to the state and federal governments for relief from the very bosses that helped make them.

In 1929, Prohibition was still the law of the land, but in Tom's Town, the clubs stayed open, and the liquor continued to flow. Jazz musicians came to find work in the Kansas City jazz clubs that thrived during the era. And many

Floodwaters in James Street, Kansas City, Kansas. *Courtesy of the Library of Congress Prints and Photographs Division (LC-USZ62-21496).*

outstanding performers (like Count Basie and Bernie Moten) launched their careers in the wide-open town. The Eighteenth and Vine area had grown from a working- and a middle-class African American neighborhood in the 1890s to a commerce and entertainment center for the segregated community in the 1920s. The Gem Theatre, Cherry Blossom Club and scores of other businesses were concentrated in the area. Jones Billiard Parlor, at East Eighteenth Street, was a hangout for Duke Ellington, Charlie Parker, Walter Page and many others. The Kansas City Monarchs baseball team even had offices nearby. At 2001 Vine, the Kansas City Workhouse tried to teach skills to and reform the prisoners who had been enlisted to build it. The town had been rebuilt after the 1903 flood, survived a horrible flu epidemic, flew through World War I and roared into the 1920s with enthusiasm.

The city was proud of its progress; its annual horse show, dubbed the American Royal, had grown from a local fair and cattle-judging contest to a major event that drew contestants from all over the country. A sketch club, started by local artists, had grown into the Kansas City Art Institute with the help of local businessman Howard Vanderslice, who purchased the land and mansion of August Meyer for the school. Alumni of the school include a long list of successful artists: Walt Disney, Mort Walker and Dennis Hopper, to name a few. Henry "Harry" Perry came to Kansas City around 1908 and brought his experience in cooking Memphis-style barbecue with him. By slow-cooking meats in a pit and creating an original rub and sauce, Perry created a Kansas City tradition. He operated out of a trolley barn at the corner of Nineteenth and Highland Streets in the African American neighborhood near Eighteenth and Vine. Perry served slow-cooked ribs on pages of newsprint for twenty-five cents per slab. Arthur Bryant and George Gates both partnered with men who had worked for Perry and expanded his legacy with their own signature sauces. All that followed was built on Perry's foundation.

The city had an exuberant spirit in those days; the town was growing with planned communities, and its people worked hard and played hard. The country club south of town and the tennis courts and parks in northeast gave the city's wealthy a place to congregate. While the town had many

Dedication of Liberty Memorial site, Kansas City, Missouri, November 1, 1921. *Courtesy of the Library of Congress Prints and Photographs Division (LC-USZ62-125644).*

new parks, the red-light district and the clubs in the Eighteenth and Vine District gave weekend revelers with smaller budgets plenty of opportunities to blow off steam. In the segregated town, there were two major baseball teams: the Kansas City Blues and the Kansas City Monarchs. The latter had some of the best players in the history of the game, like Satchel Paige, Jackie Robinson and Buck O'Neil.

In 1920, a group of the city's leading citizens, including J.C. Nichols, William Volker, James Madison Kemper and landscape architect George Kessler, chose R.A. Long to head the effort to build a memorial to those who served in the Great War. Within a year, Long and the community had raised the money they needed, and a crowd of two hundred thousand gathered at the groundbreaking ceremony. Vice President Calvin Coolidge spoke at the event, and dignitaries, including Marshal Foch and General John Pershing, were in attendance. The entire community pitched in, and the 180-foot-high Liberty Memorial was completed in 1926. At the unveiling, then-president Calvin Coolidge spoke again, and Queen Marie of Romania was in attendance. The National World War I Museum at Liberty Memorial is both a local and national treasure, and it was built through the efforts of all levels of Kansas City's society.

The Great Depression had a profound effect on Tom's Town, but the tougher things got, the harder the city's leaders fought back. When other cities were cutting back, Kansas City set forth on an ambitious building spree that provided much-needed jobs and improved the city's ability to serve the community. The city's Ten-Year Plan was the creation of boss Tom

Above: Kansas City Horse Show, circa 1905. *Courtesy of the Library of Congress Prints and Photographs Division (LOT 5784 no. 2 (OSF)).*

Left: City Hall, elevated view, south elevation, 414 East Twelfth Street, Kansas City, Missouri. *Courtesy of the Library of Congress Prints and Photographs Division (HABS MO,48-KANCI,4—7).*

Union Station, circa 1903, Kansas City, Missouri. *Courtesy of the Library of Congress Prints and Photographs Division (LC-DIG-highsm-04193).*

Pendergast, city manager H.F. McElroy and Conrad Mann, president of the Kansas City Chamber of Commerce. A $50 million bond was passed in 1931 to fund the plan. The project improved Kansas City's trafficways, sewer system, waterworks, parks, postal services, police and firefighting equipment, street signs and pedestrian walkways. Landmarks built under the plan included the Municipal Auditorium, city hall, police headquarters and the Jackson County Courthouse.

Boss Tom Pendergast controlled much of the city but not all of it. Prohibition had extended the reach of criminal gangs, and the Great Depression had made a new and more violent criminal class that would often align with or try to take over the old political machines in the city. In 1933, in an attempt to free prisoner Frank Nash, a group of gangsters, led by Vernon Miller, attacked a group of officers who were transporting Nash to Fort Leavenworth. The shooting spree took place in Union Station, and it came to be known as the Union Station Massacre. The FBI and local police force were woefully outgunned, but Nash was killed in the machinegun spray that hit the group. J. Edgar Hoover used the incident to expand the power of the FBI and arm its agents. The corrupting influence of the mob and the machine led to a wave of reform that eventually overturned even Boss Tom, but his mark remains all over the city.

KANSAS CITY JAZZ MUSEUM

1616 East Eighteenth Street
Kansas City, Missouri 64108
www.americanjazzmuseum.org

MARR SOUND ARCHIVE

800 East Fifty-First Street
Kansas City, Missouri 64110
www.library.umkc.edu/marr

During the 1920s and 1930s, Kansas City's African American musicians created a new tune, a unique blend of jazz and the blues, through experimentation and improvisation. Displaced musicians came to Kansas City, where they could sing after they'd been forbidden in other cities. The historic district and world-class museum document a time when dance halls, cabarets, speakeasies and even honky-tonks and juke joints fostered the development of this new musical style: Kansas City jazz. If you want access to more music, Kansas City is fortunate to be the home of the MARR Sound Archives.

EIGHTEENTH AND VINE DISTRICT

East Eighteenth and Vine Streets
Kansas City, Missouri 64108
www.18vinekc.com; kcparks.org/places/charlie-parker-memorial

The *New York Times* called this historic district "the renowned mecca of black politics and entertainment in the city." It's more than that—it's the cradle of Kansas City's African American experience and a political pocket that reminds us that black people were segregated to this area (and other red-lined neighborhoods) until the mid-1960s. The Charlie "Bird" Parker statue at the corner of Eighteenth and Vine Streets invites visitors to the historic district. The Gem Theater (1615 East Eighteenth Street) and the Mutual Musicians Foundation (1823 Highland Avenue) are just two of the attractions you can find in the district. Other sites in this district are highlighted separately in this guide.

Negro Leagues Baseball Museum

1616 East Eighteenth Street
Kansas City, Missouri 64108
www.nlbm.com

Hit a grand slam while you're in Kansas City and make a short stop at "the world's only museum dedicated to preserving and celebrating the rich history of African American baseball and its impact on the social advancement of America." In the 1800s, black players were allowed to play on military, college and company teams, but they were eventually forced to segregate in the early 1900s. For the next fifty years, they played in leagues of their own. While the civil rights movement got a "hit" in 1945, when the Brooklyn Dodgers recruited Jackie Robinson from the Kansas City Monarchs, his recruitment was a "strike" against the Negro Leagues, which folded in the early 1960s.

Kansas City Mafia Tour and Kansas City Tour Company

816-286-5298
www.kansascitytorucompany.com

It must be said that Kansas City was a wide-open town through the 1930s. Even with the Clean Sweep Election of 1940, which ousted the Pendergast regime, there was still an underground of mob and gangster activity in the city. Today, you can read books and watch productions about this activity from a safe distance, but local historian Eric Stafford offers a professionally guided tour for an up-close and personal experience. Stafford also hosts a Be Bop tour, a Black History tour and a Civil Rights tour by streetcar, so there's no need to "forgetta bout it."

Kansas City Workhouse Castle

2001 Vine Street
Kansas City, Missouri 64108

Two of the city's oldest buildings, located near the Eighteenth and Vine District, have been in ruins for decades and look like they came right out

Kansas City workhouse, Twenty-First and Vine Streets, Kansas City, Missouri. *Courtesy of David W. Jackson, orderlypackrat.com.*

of the Middle Ages—technically, they were designed in the Romanesque Revival style. But the 1890s buildings, with great views of the downtown skyline, are being brought back to life, as is the formerly segregated Wheatley Provident Hospital in the historic Eighteenth and Vine District. In the past, petty offenders worked off their sentences and fines at the workhouse; women sewed prison uniforms and men labored for the city's Public Works Department. To find other castles in and around Kansas City, search for Vaile Mansion, Sauer Castle and Tiffany Castle on the internet.

NATIONAL WORLD WAR I MUSEUM AT LIBERTY MEMORIAL

2 Memorial Drive
Kansas City, Missouri 64108
www.theworldwar.org

This designated National Historic Landmark was our country's official World War I museum and memorial. In 1919, Kansas Citians raised more than $2.5 million in ten days (the equivalent of $34 million over one hundred years later). Groundbreaking ribbons were cut in 1921, in front of one hundred thousand spectators (they didn't have television, so this was a prime-time event). In 1926, the completed Liberty Memorial was dedicated by president Calvin Coolidge and more than 150, 000 attendees. Today, visitors can enjoy a variety of spectacular permanent and temporary exhibits, and they shouldn't miss a ride to the top of the Liberty Memorial Tower—it's worth the price of admission and beats anything you can watch on television.

Pendergast Haunts and Tom Pendergast's Private Residence

5650 Ward Parkway
Kansas City, Missouri 64113

Tom Pendergast Political Headquarters, 1927–1939

1908 Main Street
Kansas City, Missouri 64108
www.pendergastkc.org

Jim Pendergast Statue

West Ninth and Jefferson Streets
www.kcparks.org/places/pendergast-james-memorial-2

Eight Pendergast siblings came into town on the coattails of their brother, James "Jim" Pendergast, a rugged character who governed with truth and courage as a city councilmember. Tom was the one who "rose" to the top, though a lingering smell that was anything but floral. But there were thorns,

Thomas J. Pendergast House, 5650 Ward Parkway. *Courtesy of the State Historical Society of Missouri, Photograph Collection (J.C. Nichols Company Scrapbooks, K0054-v14p144-01).*

too. The Pendergast boys reined a mob-like, Tammany Hall–style regime. Kansas City's biggest political boss was literally a big guy, as well, but experts summed him up perfectly when they said:

> *His open alliance with hardened criminals, his cynical subversion of the democratic process, his monarchistic style of living, his increasingly insatiable gambling habit, his grasping for a business empire and his promotion of Kansas City as a wide-open town with every kind of vice imaginable, combined with his professed compassion for the poor and very real role as city builder, made him bigger than life, difficult to characterize.*

CITY HALL AND JACKSON COUNTY COURTHOUSE

414 East Twelfth Street
Kansas City, Missouri 64106
www.kcmo.gov/city-hall

The same Great Depression–era bond issue built both the Art Deco Jackson County Courthouse and city hall across the street from one another in downtown Kansas City. At the same time, the city was also conducting major road and bridge projects. The last-known surviving bridge from this time is the iron Red Bridge, which spans the Big Blue River at Red Bridge Road. If you visit city hall, be sure to go to the observation deck for a fantastic view of the city from above.

FEDERAL RESERVE BANK OF KANSAS CITY AND THE MONEY MUSEUM

1 Memorial Drive
Kansas City, Missouri 64198
www.kansascityfed.org/moneymuseum

This museum provides visitors with a fascinating look at their money, no matter their age. In other words, it is cool for youths and adults alike. There, visitors can learn all they want to know about the United States' economy and the federal reserve on the museum's tour. The museum is also home to historic coins and bills, a huge cash vault and more.

HISTORIC TRUMAN JACKSON COUNTY COURTHOUSE

112 West Lexington Avenue
Independence, Missouri 64050
www.jacksongov.org/586/county-history

The Great Depression of the 1930s left millions of people across the country unemployed. Kansas City was fortunate to have both federal relief programs and a robust county works program, which voters passed as a major bond issue to keep folks working on civic structures. Harry S. Truman, then a county legislator, was at the heart of the county works program. The historic Truman Jackson County Courthouse in Independence Square was remodeled in 1933 to its present incarnation; the modern structure includes remnants of several previous courthouses, including almost all of the original structure from 1836 (the first permanent brick courthouse in Jackson County). Visitors should arrange to take a guided tour of the courthouse, during which they can stand inside the 1836 nucleus of the building—the original Jackson County Circuit Courtroom. Just one block to the south of the courthouse, at 107 West Kansas Avenue, is the 1827 Log Courthouse, which was hewn by African American slave labor to be used as a "temporary structure."

Jackson County's Historic Truman Courthouse, Independence Square, Independence, Missouri. *Courtesy of Paul Kirkman.*

Read More

Black Baseball in Kansas City, by Sammy J. Miller and Larry Lester
Black Hand Strawman (film), by Terence O'Malley
A City Divided: The Racial Landscape of Kansas City, by Sherry Schirmer
Confidence Restored: The History of the Tenth District's Federal Reserve Bank, by Tim Todd
Gangland Wire (film), by Gary Jenkin
The Grand Barbecue: A Celebration of the History, Places, Personalities and Techniques of Kansas City Barbecue, by Doug Worgul
Harry S. Truman: His Life and Times, by Brian Burnes
Kansas City: 1940, by John Simonson
The Kansas City Monarchs, by Janet Bruce-Campbell
Lest the Ages Forget: Kansas City's Liberty Memorial, by Derek Donovan
The Mafia and the Machine, by Frank Hayde
Mobsters in our Midst, by William Ouseley
The Negro Leagues Book, edited by Dick Clark and Larry Lester
Open City, by William Ouseley
Paris of the Plains: Kansas City from Doughboys to Expressways, by John Simonson
Pendergast!, by Lawrence H. Larsen and Nancy J. Hulston
Rags to Be-Bop: The Sounds of Kansas City Music, 1890–1945, by Chuck Haddix
Results of County Planning: Jackson County, Missouri, by Harry S. Truman and the Jackson County Court
Some of My Best Friends are Black: The Strange Story of Integration in America, by Tanner Colby
Take Up the Black Man's Burden: Kansas City's African American Communities, 1865–1939, by Charles E. Coulter
Wide-Open Town: Kansas City in the Pendergast Era, by Diane Mutti Burke, Jason Roe and John Herron
Winding the Clock on the Independence Square: Jackson County's Historic Truman Courthouse, by David W. Jackson

8
THE SENATOR FROM PENDERGAST

Kansas City survived political scandal, economic hardship and criminal activity, but a greater challenge was just around the corner. With another war on the horizon, the town that Tom built produced another unlikely product. Harry Truman had started down a number of paths as a young man. He was bookish and had to wear glasses, he took business classes after high school and he worked for a railroad and bank for a while. He then spent eleven years working on his family's farm before serving in the Great War. Truman ended up back in Independence, Missouri, after World War I; he tried and failed to make a haberdashery on Twelfth Street in Kansas City successful. When Boss Tom's nephew Jim Pendergast sought a job for his old army buddy, neither could have known that the failed haberdasher and farmer would ascend all the way to the presidency during World War II.

Boss Tom wasn't overly impressed with Truman, but Harry worked well in Jackson County politics and eventually became a county judge; in an administrative position, like county commissioner, he pushed along the agenda of the machine, with infrastructure projects that benefited the community and the Pendergast concrete business. After serving a couple terms as county judge, Truman turned to the machine for its support during his run for a higher position. He was turned down. In 1934, Truman was eventually tapped as Pendergast's fifth choice to run for senator. He had been an active member of veterans' groups and was well known in the state, and with the machine's backing, he won the position. "The Senator from

Pendergast" was hardly a fair eponym for Harry Truman. While in office, he let the machine make decisions concerning patronage, but he said he voted his conscience on all other matters. Truman was a New Deal Democrat who distrusted big business and whose personal political beliefs aligned well with those of the Democratic machine in Kansas City.

Harry S. Truman, thirty-third president of the United States. *Photograph by Walters in Seattle, courtesy of the Library of Congress, Prints and Photographs Division (LC-USZ62-99665).*

In spite of Boss Tom being arrested and jailed, Truman's personal reputation was saved enough for him to be reelected in 1940. In his second term, Truman went after waste in military contracts and received a chairmanship in the Committee on Military Affairs Subcommittee on War Mobilization. His work investigating waste and fraud in military contracts saved the country billions of dollars and landed him a spot on *Time Magazine*'s cover.

President Franklin Delano Roosevelt's vice president Henry Wallace, was considered a liability in the 1944 election, so he found an alternative candidate in Harry Truman. The two won the election; however, Roosevelt's health was failing, and Truman had only served as vice president for eighty-two days before Roosevelt died. Truman was faced with the task of taking the reins of the U.S. government while the country was still fighting a horrific war. He had to both heal and lead a nation that was thrown into disarray by the passing of Roosevelt. In a matter of weeks, Truman was informed that the United States had developed the atomic bomb. After the Allies' victory in Europe, a series of hard-fought battles moved the Allies closer to the main island of Japan. But the Japanese refused to surrender under terms of the Potsdam Agreement, and Truman was faced with the decision of either using an atomic weapon or mounting an invasion that he was told, according to military estimates, could take a year to complete and result in 250,000 to 500,000 U.S. casualties. A number of historians have criticized his decision, but the majority of Americans at the time were relieved to know their loved ones would not be at war and at risk for another year.

Kansas City celebrated the end World War II, mourned its dead and helped reelect its hometown president. The war years had put thousands of women and minorities to work, building planes, amphibious vehicles, bullets and bombs. The end of the war meant an end of the wartime economy. Many of the returning soldiers started families and needed homes. Kansas City grew its borders, at least in part, to keep the new subdivisions inside its tax base.

In 1951, the Missouri River once more asserted its control over life in the city with a massive flood. The flooding started in Kansas, on the tributaries to the Kaw River, and it then made its way to Kansas City, first submerging homes in the West Bottoms, Argentine and Armourdale. The flooding destroyed the stockyards, causing hundreds of millions of dollars' worth of damage along the way. Over one million acres of land in Kansas and Missouri were inundated, half a million people were displaced and both state capitols were flooded, as were two hundred other towns and cities in the river's path. When the crest from the Kaw hit the Missouri River, it caused the Missouri to rise fourteen feet above flood stage—the river's flow was ten times faster than its normal rate. The Trans World Airlines (TWA) overhaul base at the Fairfax Airport was destroyed, precipitating the move of the company's operations to Platte County and the eventual construction of the Mid-Continent International Airport (MCI, or Kansas City International Airport). The stockyards never fully recovered from the blow, and the rise in air and car travel, combined with the decline of the stockyards, hit the railroads and Union Station hard.

For many, World War II put life on hold, and at the end of the war, the housing and baby boom came with an increased demand for the consumer goods that had to be foregone during the war. Radio was still king, but it was being supplanted by television as the dominant media in the growing communities. Early on, the movie industry chose Kansas City as a central point from which it would ship its features across the country, and the city soon became one of Hollywood's largest distribution centers. Film Row occupied nearly twenty buildings in a four-block area of the Crossroads District. MGM, 20th Century Fox, Warner Brothers, Paramount and United Artists all kept offices there. Companies that did business with the film industry, like Manley Popcorn, also set up shop in Kansas City. Studios were busily cranking out light fare for the millions of baby boomer kids, and local television stations were catering to them as well, with shows like *Torey and Friends* and *Whizzo the Clown* topping the bill.

The J.C. Nichols Fountain, near the Kansas City Country Club Plaza, Kansas City, Missouri. *Courtesy of the Library of Congress Prints and Photographs Division (LC-DIG-highsm- 04402).*

The contrast between life in the suburbs and life in the city grew steadily during the 1950s. While many white people moved into the suburbs, Kansas City was segregated, and the majority of African Americans were shut out of the new suburban communities. The election of Dwight D. Eisenhower to the presidency ushered in a period of rapid growth, as the United States had the only industrial base that hadn't been compromised or destroyed by warfare. The construction of Interstates 70, 435 and 35 started in the mid-1950s (and it seems like it hasn't stopped since). Many of the women who had entered the workforce during the war were married and became full-time housewives—as their mothers and grandmothers before them. But many didn't or couldn't—or wouldn't. For many, the post–World War II era were the good old days of "I like Ike," Elvis and Christmas lights on the Country Club Plaza, but for others in the downtown area, there was a sense that life was leaving the city behind.

HARRY S. TRUMAN FARM HOME

12301 Blue Ridge Boulevard
Grandview, Missouri 64030
www.nps.gov/hstr

It was Truman's maternal grandfather, Solomon Young, who built the family's farm in the 1860s. Truman's grandmother, when she was widowed in her late eighties, was left to run the six-hundred-acre farm on her own, so his parents moved to the farm to help out in 1905—Truman followed the next year. Harry lived and worked on the farm from 1906 to 1917. The home didn't have electricity or indoor plumbing, and Harry shared a bedroom with his brother and the farmhands. In those days, most farm work was not mechanized, and Harry earned his keep through hard work. After his father passed away, Harry was left with the responsibility of running the farm, and he kept it going until he went into active service during World War I. Today, the Harry S. Truman Farm Home is operated by the National Park Service. The home is not currently open for tours, but the grounds are open daily. If there aren't any cards with the information on site, call 585-672-2611, and dial stops 1 through 8, starting at the house and walking around the grounds, for a self-tour.

HARRY S. AND BESS TRUMAN HOME (NOT THE OFFICIAL NAME, BUT THE WOMAN DESERVES CREDIT.)

219 North Delaware Street
Independence, Missouri 64050
www.nps.gov/hstr

The Victorian home originally belonged to Truman's mother-in-law, Madge Wallace, but for the first thirty-three years of his marriage, Truman lived there with his beloved wife, Bess. The couple also raised their daughter, Margaret, and endured Wallace's criticisms there. Wallace wasn't Truman's biggest fan, and since it was her house, Harry had to bite his lip—a lot. The National Park Service preserves the over fifty thousand artifacts related to the Truman family (including used shoestrings that were hoarded in a shoe box). History lovers in Missouri should visit the home in Independence, Missouri, "the center of the world," as Harry called it. While they're there,

Truman Home, 219 North Delaware Street, Independence, Missouri. *Courtesy of Paul Kirkman.*

visitors can bop down the street for a soda or ice cream at Clinton's at Maple and Main, where Harry had his first job. This was just across the street from the county courthouse, where, years later, he got his start in politics.

HARRY S. TRUMAN PRESIDENTIAL LIBRARY AND MUSEUM

500 West US Highway 24
Independence, Missouri 64050
www.trumanlibrary.gov

If visitors can wait to visit the gift shop last, they should start their tour with the library's fifteen-minute video program that was made by Academy Award–winning director Charles Guggenheim and narrated by Jason Robards. "It traces the story of Harry Truman's family, boyhood, life on the farm, courtship of Bess, World War I service, business ventures, political career, association with the Pendergast machine, Senate career and selection as vice president." The library and museum cover, with detail and care, these and other topics from a truly remarkable presidential administration. Visitors can even walk through a replica of Truman's Oval Office. And before they leave, visitors should turn around again and take in the museum's expansive mural that was painted by Thomas Hart Benton—they'll be primed for the next site in this chapter's line up.

THOMAS HART BENTON HOME AND STUDIO STATE HISTORIC SITE

3616 Belleview Avenue
Kansas City, Missouri 64111
www.mostateparks.com

Truman's friend Tom Benton. was an exceptional Missouri artist; he was a painter, muralist, sculptor, lecturer and writer. He came from a family of politicians, but his passions were art and teaching. He taught at the Kansas City Art Institute from 1935 to 1941, and he was known for his anti-modernist and regionalist art. His life's story is present in both his home and in his paintings. His cantankerous spirit may also remain in his studio, which is kept just as it was the day he died there, in 1975. Both Benton and Truman were criticized and praised for their regional pride and stubbornness. Hopefully, through touring the spaces in which these men once made differences in the world, visitors will come to appreciate the exceptional qualities in each of them that built their legacies. To view more of Mr. Benton's art, visit the Nelson-Atkins Museum of Art—ask for Persephone.

HISTORIC KANSAS CITY GARMENT DISTRICT MUSEUM

800 and 801 Broadway Boulevard
Kansas City, Missouri 64105
www.kcparks.org/places/historic-garment-district-museum-of-kansas-city

Fashion and architecture come together in a stylish museum in downtown Kansas City. In the early 1900s, the dry goods industry's appetite for quality clothing was whetted when garment manufacturers took over their spaces in the now-historic district in the National Register of Historic Places. What

Sewing machine at the Kansas City Garment District Museum. *Courtesy of David W. Jackson, coauthor of* We Were Hanging by a Thread: Kansas City Garment District Pieces the Past Together.

developed was a garment district that was tailored to a wide and diverse midwestern market. Did you know that Kansas City's once-renowned industry was so successful that one out of every seven women in the United States wore garments made in Kansas City? In fact, factories manufacturing coats and suits in Kansas City were the second-largest producers in the United States. By the 1980s, however, the industry had imploded due to changing markets, globalization and the advent of big box stores. The only fortunate outcome for this change in the Garment District was that a fantastic museum with a robust garment collection of "Made in Kansas" fashions was made available to the public. Founded in 2002 by former fashion designer Ann Brownfield and garment manufacturer Harvey Fried, the museum has been turned over to the custody of the Garment District Museum, which is located in the historic Poindexter Building, next to the Kansas City Museum.

WORLD WAR II BOMBER BUILDER'S MONUMENT

631 North 126th Street
Bonner Springs, Kansas 66012
www.wycokck.org/wycomuseum b-25history.org/history/monument.htm

During World War II, fifty thousand Kansas Citians—mostly women, as men were serving in the military—built 6,608 B-25 bombers in the Fairfax District of Kansas City, Kansas. This era gave birth to Rosie the Riveter and Winnie the Welder. The B-25 bomber plant in Kansas City, with over one million square feet of productive space, stood on the northwest corner of Kindleberger and Fairfax Roads. A monument was dedicated on May 2, 1998, to commemorate those industrious Americans of the Greatest Generation; today, it stands outside of the Wyandotte County Museum. It's an exemplary site worth exploring.

B-25 bombers lined up at North American Aviation Inc., almost ready for their first test flights, circa 1942, Kansas City, Kansas. *Courtesy of the Library of Congress Prints and Photographs Division (LC-DIG-fsac-1a35290).*

KANSAS CITY COUNTRY CLUB PLAZA

4706 Broadway Boulevard
Kansas City, Missouri 64112
816-753-0100
www.countryclubplaza.com

In the early 1920s, developers became married to the idea of individuals driving to shopping and dining destinations in their own, newfangled horseless carriages—or cars. The union formed the nation's first outdoor shopping mall, which was designed around cars in 1923, and was set amid what seemed to be a replica of Seville, Spain. For decades, the plaza has been a premier shopping destination for Kansas Citians, especially during the holidays. Today, the mall is home to boutique stores, restaurants, hotels, statues and fountains. If you are in Kansas City for the year-end holidays, be sure to experience the plaza's Season of Lights tradition; it was started in 1930, and today, the fifteen-block plaza is blazoned with glimmering, jewel-colored lights.

NATIONAL AIRLINE HISTORY MUSEUM

201 Northwest Lou Holland Drive
Kansas City, Missouri 64116
816-421-3401
www.airlinehistory.org

TWA MUSEUM

10 Richards Road
Kansas City, Missouri 64116
816-234-1011
www.twamuseum.com

At Kansas City's Wheeler Downtown Airport, visitors may climb aboard this unique find in Kansas City, which was opened in the 1990s and is located in Hangar 9. There, visitors can relive the golden age of propeller-driven passenger aircraft through rare photographs, artifacts, uniforms, galley items, equipment and aircraft, including one of the few remaining Lockheed Super Constellations. The TWA Museum is three hundred meters down the runway from the National Airline History Museum. Before they take off, visitors shouldn't miss taxying by the historic TWA Headquarters Building, which is topped with a rocket (an engineering feat in itself), at 1735 Baltimore Avenue.

Read More

The Country Club District of Kansas City, by Ladene Morton
Harry S. Truman Home: Harry S. Truman National Historic Site, Independence, Missouri, by Sarah Olson
Harry S. Truman: His Life and Times, by Brian Burnes
J.C. Nichols and the Shaping of Kansas City by William S. Worley
Nelly Don: A Stitch in Time, by Terence O'Malley
Off the Record: The Private Papers of Harry S. Truman, by Harry S. Truman and Robert H Ferrell
Power, Money and Women: Words to the Wise from Harry S. Truman, by Niel M. Johnson
Thomas Hart Benton, by Thomas Hart Benton
Thomas Hart Benton: An American Original, by Henry Adams
Truman, by David McCullough
TWA: Kansas City's Hometown Airline, by Julius Karash and Rick Montgomery
We Were Hanging by a Thread: Kansas City Garment District Pieces the Past Together, by Ann Brownfield and David W. Jackson
Winding the Clock on the Independence Square: Jackson County's Historic Truman Courthouse, by David W. Jackson

9
THE FUTURE OF OUR PAST

The widespread and rapid technological and cultural change that has taken place in the United States since the 1960s has left its mark on every aspect of life in Kansas City. The entrance of women into every level of the workforce, as well as the integration of military units during and after World War II, brought a renewed vision of hope for large sectors of the city's populace, who had formerly had little economic or political power.

KCI airport and Interstates 70, 435 and 35 connected the city with the rest of the United States and the world. The Country Club Plaza was the first automobile-oriented mall in the world, but it wouldn't be the last, as suburban sprawl created more and more communities that were independent and self-contained. The first multiplex movie theater was built at Ward Parkway by AMC in 1963.

In 1961, Kansas City inventor, entrepreneur and teacher Marion Trozzolo introduced the Teflon "Happy Pan" to Americans for the first time. Following his service in World War II, Trozzolo went to college in Chicago and moved to Kansas City, Missouri, in 1951 to begin his work as a professor of business administration and economics at Rockhurst University. In 1957, he opened Laboratory Plasticware Fabricators and began producing plastic-coated scientific utensils, including a Teflon-coated magnetic stirring rod. He eventually experimented with coating pans, and E.I. DuPont De Nemours and Company executives backed his 1961 introduction of the Teflon coated "Happy Pan." He continued to market the pan until he sold the company in 1972, and in the 1980s, he sold Teflon-coated mementos in honor of Ronald Reagan (nicknamed the Teflon president). He also donated a Teflon coating for the fence around the Harry S. Truman's home in Independence. An original Happy Pan is now part of the collection at the Smithsonian Institution.

Trozzolo was a fan of the City Market area and began buying its homes, old buildings and surrounding property. Over the years, he purchased over thirty buildings. By the early 1970s, the area housed a mix of shops and restaurants, and the River Quay became a destination. By 1974, it had grown to include over eighty shops and restaurants, which attracted thousands of people who came to the "new" entertainment district. Trozzolo imported three red double-decker buses from Great Britain and ran bus routes through town, promoting and encouraging people to visit the City Market.

Unfortunately, among the area's business owners were competing members of Kansas City's organized crime families. A series of killings and the bombing of three buildings in the River Quay laid waste to the plans to revitalize the area at that time. The negative publicity added to downtown's woes, as the growth to the north of the river and south of the city accelerated. The city continued to annex land and expand its tax base, but it was twenty years before the population base in the city grew organically again. Life in the suburbs, however, was a different story. New neighborhoods were popping up all along the highways and roads heading out of town; these small towns would become small cities over the course of a few years, and the city limits of one would extend over the farmland in between, right up against the next town over.

The rapid growth of a youth-driven culture, which came with the baby boom, sent traditional marketers back to the drawing board. In 1977, McDonald's introduced the Happy Meal to Kansas City; this was two years before the rest of the country got a toy with its burger.

The division and change that characterized the civil rights movement and Vietnam War era came to Kansas City as well. In 1968, a student protest over the city's failure to close schools for the funeral of Dr. Martin Luther King Jr. was dispersed by the police with tear gas, which led to a large number of adults in the community protesting the police action—this protest eventually devolved into riots.

From the war years forward, women and minorities, including members of the LGBTQ+ community, all were moved toward greater participation in the political process, and each sought an equal place at the table. The city has had mixed luck when responding to the needs of its diverse population. In the 1970s, the urban renewal movement was ostensibly meant to

McDonald's *Star Trek* Meal. *Courtesy of the Library of Congress Prints and Photographs Division (LC-DIG-ppmsca-57582).*

help the city's poor, but it destroyed many of the city's older buildings while perpetuating segregation and breaking up older communities. The realization in the 1980s that many of the city's historic landmarks were at risk led to the revitalization of historical societies and preservation efforts.

On July 17, 1981, around 1,600 people gathered at the newly completed Hyatt Regency Hotel in Kansas City, Missouri, for a tea dance. A band played, cocktails flowed and people dressed in their finest to dance while others watched from the walkways above. Suddenly, two thirty-two-ton skywalks collapsed. The fourth-story walkway went first and fell on top of the second-story walkway, causing both to collapse onto the lobby floor. In the horrible event, 114 people were killed and 200 were injured. Some thirty years later, the Skywalk Memorial Plaza was finally built on a hillside at the corner of Twenty-Second Street and Gillham Road. At the center of the memorial is an abstract metallic sculpture by artist Rita Blitt. Titled *Sending Love*, the sculpture was made to resemble two people dancing. The pedestal

Soldiers and Sailors Memorial Building, Route 69, Kansas City, Kansas. *Courtesy of the Library of Congress Prints and Photographs Division (LC-DIG-mrg-03963).*

of the sculpture displays the names of the 114 people who were killed in the collapse. From the 1830s cholera epidemic to floods, fire and disaster, Kansas City has survived, thrived and remembered to pay homage to the citizens it has lost.

Since the mid-1990s, the city's population has made a comeback after loft apartments were developed in old buildings and improvements were made to the city's transportation. A younger community has begun to reclaim the parts of the city that had been in decline for decades. The Power and Light District and Sprint Center have created new venues for concerts and celebrations downtown, and they have put the area back on the tour map of performing stars, conventions and athletic events.

The Border War has never really stopped in Kansas City, as the city is very competitive when it comes to sports, especially basketball. Ever since 1898, when James Naismith (the inventor of the game) became the head coach at Kansas University (KU) and Phog Allen (from Independence, Missouri) started playing for the Kansas City Athletic Club (1905), the sport has had a strong following in the area. Naismith coached Allen at KU, and Allen went on to coach at the university for fifty seasons. He retired with the most wins of any coach in college basketball history at the time (746). The University of Kansas and University of Missouri (MU) have met on the court nearly three hundred times, with KU handily racking up the most wins (MU fans are quick to note that their football team has bested KU more often than not on the gridiron).

OWENS-ROGERS MUSEUM

100 West Moore Street
Independence, Missouri 64050
www.owensrogersmuseum.org

There's a small touch of Hollywood in Kansas City; it is the birthplace of famed actress, dancer and singer Ginger Rogers, who was born Virginia Katherine to William E. McMath and Lela E. (Owens) McMath on July 16, 1911. In January 1920, nine-year-old Virginia Leibrand (Ginger Rogers) was living at 504 East Eighth Street in Kansas City with her twice-divorced mother, who was, by then, a veteran World War I U.S. Marine Corps sergeant (one of the first ten "Marinettes" to enlist) who had become a scriptwriter, or "scenario writer," for a film company. In May 1911, Ginger's mother married her fourth and final husband, insurance agent John Logan Rogers, and the family moved to Texas. Ginger's earliest reviewer wrote, in January 1926:

> *It is rare that Galvestonians have had occasion to meet across the footlights as winsome a youngster as Ginger Rogers, late of Fort Worth, but whose talent and genial personality will soon claim as home the entire continent. Not only is she a Charlestoner of ability, but her charm and refreshing self-poise in a youngster of fourteen years immediately stamps her as one with whom the world will yet reckon.*

Though the Rogers separated in 1928, Ginger kept her stepfather's surname to use in her glimmering stage and screen career. At the time, Kansas City wasn't just one of the largest distribution hubs in the country; it also exported some of Hollywood's greatest stars. Visitors should travel to the Crossroads Arts District at Eighteenth Street, between Wyandotte and Central Streets, in the heart of Film Row to find Kansas City's own Walk of Fame. The walkway features actual stars that represent some of the city's most beloved native celebrities, including Joan Crawford, Walt Disney, Jean Harlow, Ginger Rogers and more.

THE CITY OF FOUNTAINS FOUNDATION

PO Box 9193
Shawnee Mission, Kansas 66201
816-842-2299
www.kcfountains.com

Kansas City's fountains were once utilitarian and served thirsty horses and dogs. Later, folks got creative and incorporated sculpture, art and architecture into the fountains. Today, there is a fountain foundation that has registered more than two hundred fountains in Kansas City, making it the "City of Fountains." The city's modern logo even includes the symbol of a fountain. The foundation, which was launched in 1973, is dedicated to restoring and building at least one fountain every year. The Women's Leadership Fountain at the corner of Ninth Street and Paseo Boulevard is the oldest surviving municipally built fountain; it dates back to 1899. However, if 1899 seems too recent for you, you should check out the Rozelle Court Fountain at the Nelson-Atkins Museum of Art. It is an ancient Italian design, which technically makes it the oldest fountain in town. When you visit the foundation's website, you'll also find a list, with pictures, of many of the city's public art sculptures.

CLENDENING HISTORY OF MEDICINE, LIBRARY AND MUSEUM, UNIVERSITY OF KANSAS MEDICAL CENTER

3901 Rainbow Avenue
Kansas City, Kansas 66160
913-588-7087
www.kumc.edu/school-of-medicine

LINDA HALL LIBRARY

5109 Cherry Street
Kansas City, Missouri 64110
816-362-4600
www.lindahall.org

If science and technology are your thing, there are at least two local institutions in Kansas City that should satisfy your penchant. The Clendening History of Medicine Museum illustrates the history of medicine in the community, including that of the staff, students and faculty members of the University of Kansas Medical Center, who shaped the future of medicine. Meanwhile, Linda Hall Library (named after Herbert Hall, of the Hall-Bartlett Grain Company's, wife, Linda) is a privately endowed library of science, engineering and technology, and it has been open to the public since April 1946. Its holdings of over 2 million items include a collection of 62,358 books and other items that were originally assembled by John Adams prior to his presidency; it was purchased from the American Academy of Arts and Sciences. The library's History of Science Collection contains more than 50,000 volumes, including rare, first editions of many landmark texts of science and technology. The oldest book in the collection is a 1472 printing of Pliny the Elder's *Naturalis Historia*.

BELTON MUSEUM AND BELTON HISTORICAL SOCIETY

512 Main Street
Belton, Missouri 64012
816-322-3977
www.beltonhistoricalsociety.org

Carrie Nation, Dale Carnegie and Harry Truman are the three big names that are associated with this modest Missouri town—this author will allow you to discover the connections. Belton is representative of the many towns and cities in the Kansas City metropolitan area that have a small, nonprofit, volunteer-run historical society or museum that is dedicated to preserving local history. Some of the towns that are not mentioned elsewhere in this guidebook include Oak Grove, Grain Valley, Blue Springs, Pleasant Hill Shawnee and Grandview. The Heritage League of Greater Kansas City helps to cross-promote its membership through a fantastic history map that you can get for free when you contact heritageleaguekc.org.

AMC WARD PARKWAY

148600 Ward Parkway
Kansas City, Missouri 64114
816-333-1300

The idea of the megaplex movie theaters that we enjoy today—and stadium seating—originated in Kansas City. The genius Stan Durwood, the CEO of the company that would later become AMC (American Multi-Cinema), developed these ideas in Kansas City. The Kansas City area's first outdoor shopping mall designed around the automobile was the Kansas City Country Club Plaza, and it was built in 1923. The Blue Ridge Mall was completed in 1958, and it was the region's first—and one of the nation's earliest—suburban shopping malls. It was originally open-air but was fully enclosed in 1971; by 2008, it was rebuilt as Blue Ridge Crossing. The Ward Parkway Center was opened in 1959, and it debuted the nation's first modern movie multiplex (originally called the AMC Twin Theaters) in 1963. By November 1991, Kansas City–based AMC Theaters had expanded to twelve theaters, and in March 1994, AMC announced the addition of ten more screens and one thousand more seats at that location, making it the country's largest movie theater. You'll have to ask them how they went from twenty-two back to the current fourteen theaters at Ward Parkway—we ran out of film, and the next movie is about to start rolling.

BLACK ARCHIVES OF MID-AMERICA AND HORACE M. PETERSON III BUILDING

1722 East Seventeenth Street
Kansas City, Missouri 64108
www.blackarchives.org

BLACK ARCHIVES MUSEUM

3406 Frederick Avenue
St. Joseph, Missouri 64506
www.stjosephmuseum.org/black-archives-museum

Kansas City's Black Archives Museum preserves and promotes the social, economic, political and cultural histories of persons of African American descent in the central United States, with particular emphasis in the Kansas City, Missouri region. The Midwest Afro-American Genealogy Interest Coalition (MAGIC) encourages those with African ancestry to discover their family histories. The Black Archives Museum in St. Joseph complements the regional coverage of black history and heritage, with a more finite focus on its fair city.

KANSAS CITY PUBLIC LIBRARY, CENTRAL LIBRARY

10 West Tenth Street
Kansas City, Missouri 64105
www.mymcpl.org

MIDWEST GENEALOGY CENTER

3440 South Lee's Summit Road
Independence, Missouri 64055
www.kclibrary.org

Today's ten library branches, which serve over 1.7 million metropolitan residents in the greater Kansas City area, were started in 1873, and the first building was organized in 1889—free and open to all. Visitors to the area should drive by the 1897 Library Building at Ninth and Locust Streets. Then, they should stop in the Central Library downtown and make their way to the fifth floor to explore one of the most comprehensive collections of Kansas City regional history conserved in the Missouri Valley Special Collections. Visitors should also not forget about the Mid-Continent Public Library System (originally the Jackson County Library before it was consolidated in 1965); it stretches across fifty-six cities in three counties and serves nearly 800,000 patrons. With thirty-one branches, the system's flagship Midwest Genealogy Center is one of the country's largest and preeminent resources for family history.

GAY AND LESBIAN ARCHIVE OF MID-AMERICA (GLAMA), LABUDDE SPECIAL COLLECTIONS, MILLER NICHOLS LIBRARY, UNIVERSITY OF MISSOURI-KANSAS CITY

800 East Fifty-First Street
Kansas City, Missouri 64110
816-235-5712
www.umkc.edu/glama

The preservation of minority history took one step forward on World AIDS Day 2009, when three local historians organized GLAMA to make accessible materials that reflect the histories of the LGBTQ+ communities of the Kansas City region. GLAMA co-founder David W. Jackson is the author of *Changing Times: Almanac and Digest of Kansas City's LGBTQIA History*, which chronicles this unique history and highlights GLAMA collections. Visitors should make an appointment to research in the growing collections, or they should donate for their posterity. Visitors should also stop by the city's first-ever LGBTQ+ history marker at the corner of Twelfth and Wyandotte Streets; the marker documents Kansas City's 1966 role in launching the modern-day gay rights movement.

JOHNSON COUNTY (KANSAS) ARTS AND HERITAGE CENTER

8788 Metcalf Avenue
Overland Park, Kansas 66212
www.jcprd.com/330/Museum

Suburban Kansas City history is the specialty of this museum, which was started in 1967, in a two-room schoolhouse. Today, the twenty-thousand-square-foot Johnson County Arts and Heritage Center includes the museum's 1950s All-Electric House.

LEILA'S HAIR MUSEUM

1333 South Noland Road
Independence, Missouri 64055
816-833-2955
www.facebook.com/Leilas-Hair-Museum and leilashairmuseum.net

Believe it or not, Kansas City has the world's only museum dedicated to hair, with hair from as long ago as the seventeenth century. The museum contains locks from the noggins of folks like Michael Jackson and Queen Victoria. If you've never seen a hair wreath (they have over six hundred of them) or jewelry made of human hair (they have over two thousand pieces), don't "cut" your vacation short—hop, clip, jump and "do it up" in Leila's Hair Museum.

NATIONAL MUSEUM OF TOYS AND MINIATURES

5235 Oak Street
Kansas City, Missouri 64112
816-235-8000
www.ktoyandminiaturemuseum.org

Unwrapped in 1982, Mary Harris Francis and Barbara Marshall's toy pipe dream has expanded to include seventy-two thousand objects displayed in thirty-three thousand square feet of state-of-the-art exhibit spaces. The national museum boasts the world's largest fine-scale miniature collection and one of the nation's largest antique toy collections on public display. This fantastic gem is not just for kids—it is for the young at heart, who seek to remember the toys of yesteryear.

RUSSELL STOVER

2814 Shawnee Mission Parkway
Fairway, Kansas 66205
913-945-2744
www.russellstover.com

While Russel was Stover's husband's name, the chocolatier started her business as Mrs. Stover's Bungalow Candies in 1923. Along the way, someone let their sweet tooth get the better of them, but whatever the name, the candy's the same: sweet, smooth, delicious and authentically Kansas City. Today, Russell Stover's candies can be found everywhere, including in Hall's Department Store (a Hallmark-adjacent company that has also been unique to Kansas City since 1910), but visitors should still check out the shop in Fairway, just west of the Kansas City Country Club Plaza.

PUPPETRY ARTS INSTITUTE

11025 East Winner Road
Independence, Missouri 64052
www.puppetryartsinstitute.org

Before they leave Candyland, visitors need to pull some strings in their Kansas City adventures and visit the Englewood area of Independence, Missouri. There, they will see the town's internationally acclaimed puppet and marionets collection, including the Hazelle Rollins Puppet Museum. Hazelle owned the world's largest puppet factory in Kansas City from 1935 to 1975—howdy doody! Visitors may also be in town for one of the museum's regular puppet shows, which are always well received. Visitors will never look at their socks in the same way. While in Englewood, visitors should paint the town red in the flourishing arts district. And they shouldn't forget to visit Vivilore, an elegant restaurant, unique events space, art gallery and antique shoppe.

THE COLLEGE BASKETBALL EXPERIENCE

1401 Grand Boulevard
Kansas City, Missouri 64106
816-949-7500
www.collegebasketballexperience.com

Don't "pass" this up. "Travel" to this world-class facility next to the grand lobby of the Sprint Center in downtown Kansas City. The museum's two floors "dribble" 41,500 square feet of everything basketball. Its "slam dunk" is the National Collegiate Basketball Hall of Fame, which highlights college basketball legends. This is a seriously fun stop in a popular area of town, and it is a family-friendly site for sports history enthusiasts. There are also team-specific halls of fame at both the Royals' and Chiefs' stadiums—for the sport history super fan.

McDONALD'S HAPPY MEAL

11700 East US 24 Highway
Independence, Missouri 64054

McDonald's drive-in restaurants debuted in Kansas City around May 1962, when McDonald's was just seven years old and had already sold over 150 million hamburgers. Ray Croc attended the opening ceremonies. The McDonald's Happy Meal—created by Kansas City advertising agency Bernstein-Rein—debuted in Kansas City in October 1977. Don't you wish you'd saved your first Happy Meal box and toy? For your trivial pursuits, the first five privately owned McDonald's franchises around Kansas City were located at 3115 Raytown Roadd (owned by Leslie L. Fink), 8020 South US 71 (owned by Lata Matas and Bud Cardiff), 4900 Swope Parkway (owned by Henry Hoffman), East Highway 40 and Hardy in Independence (owned by Paul K. Hauffman and Robert K Jones) and 11700 East US 24 in Sugar Creek (owned by Ron Wiegand and Don Umbach). The last of these golden-arch McDonald's is the only one that is still serving. Don't you deserve a break today?

Read More

Black Tie White Tie (film), by Lyle Gibson
Changing Times: Almanac and Digest of Kansas City's LGBTQIA History, by David W. Jackson
The City of Fountains: Kansas City's Legacy of Beauty and Motion, by Roy Inman
Double Entendre, by Patrick C. Byrne
Fountains of Kansas City: A History and Love Affair, by Sherry a*Ginger: My Story*, by Ginger Rogers
Hazelle and Her Marionettes, by Mike Joly
Highlights from the Collection of the National Museum of Toys and Miniatures, by the National Museum of Toys and Miniatures
Kansas City (Black America Series), by Delia C. Gillis
Kansas City: Mecca of the New Negro, by Sonny Gibson
Saturday Matinee in Olde KC, by Chris Wilborn
Steptoe: A Step Above the Plaza (film), by Rodney M. Thompson
Toy and Miniature Museum of Kansas City, by Tom and Joyce Moulis
Your Kansas City and Mine, by William H. Young

INDEX

N

O

P

Q

R

S

T

U

V

W

ABOUT THE AUTHOR

Paul Kirkman is the author of *The Battle of Westport: Missouri's Great Confederate Raid* (The History Press, 2011), *Forgotten Tales of Kansas City* (The History Press, 2012), *Missouri Outlaws: Bandits, Rebels & Rogues* (The History Press, 2018) and coauthor of *Lockdown: Outlaws, Lawmen, and Frontier Justice in Jackson County, Missouri* (with David Jackson, Jackson County Historical Society, 2012). Paul has a bachelor's degree in history from Columbia College and is a former speaker for the State Historical Society of Missouri Speakers' Bureau. He lives in Independence, Missouri, with his wife, Shawn, and his grandsons, Benjamin and Samuel Carey. His daughter, Shannon Kirkman, is currently a student at Kansas University.